SpringerBriefs in Psychology

SpringerBriefs present concise summaries of cutting-edge research and practical applications across a wide spectrum of fields. Featuring compact volumes of 50 to 125 pages, the series covers a range of content from professional to academic. Typical topics might include:

- A timely report of state-of-the-art analytical techniques
- A bridge between new research results as published in journal articles and a contextual literature review
- A snapshot of a hot or emerging topic
- An in-depth case study or clinical example
- A presentation of core concepts that readers must understand to make independent contributions

SpringerBriefs in Psychology showcase emerging theory, empirical research, and practical application in a wide variety of topics in psychology and related fields. Briefs are characterized by fast, global electronic dissemination, standard publishing contracts, standardized manuscript preparation and formatting guidelines, and expedited production schedules.

More information about this series at http://www.springer.com/series/10143

Nasima MH Carrim · J. Alewyn Nel · Riana Schoeman

Occupational Stress in South African Work Culture

Examining the Work Locus of Control of Managers

Springer

Nasima MH Carrim
Human Resource Management Department
University of Pretoria
Pretoria, South Africa

J. Alewyn Nel
Human Resource Management Department
University of Pretoria
Pretoria, South Africa

Riana Schoeman
University of Pretoria
Pretoria, South Africa

ISSN 2192-8363 ISSN 2192-8371 (electronic)
SpringerBriefs in Psychology
ISBN 978-981-33-6396-0 ISBN 978-981-33-6397-7 (eBook)
https://doi.org/10.1007/978-981-33-6397-7

This Springer imprint is published by the registered company Springer Nature Singapore Pte Ltd.
The registered company address is: 152 Beach Road, #21-01/04 Gateway East, Singapore 189721, Singapore

Summary

The workplace is evidently one of the greatest causes of stress. Business executives and managers have an inherent responsibility to identify and appropriately manage occupational stress. A stress-filled workplace can have a dire effect on organisations as a whole and with working conditions changing because of the COVID-19, these effects are becoming even more important. The rationale for this book is to explore avenues for organisations to better understand the origins of occupational stress and enable their managerial employees to effectively manage their stress levels by means of work locus of control as a personality variable. The book also aims to illustrate an in-depth perspective into occupational stress by identifying stressors within and outside the organisation that are the cause of high stress levels. Not much is known about the relationship between occupational stress and work locus of control. In the current global COVID-19 crisis and the effects thereof on the economy, it is imperative for managerial employees to perform their tasks at an optimal level. Hence, the focus of this book in exploring the impact that work locus of control has on occupational stress. The aim of the book is to assist organisations in understanding the impact that work locus of control orientation has on the perception of occupational stress, and in doing so instil a culture of internally orientated managers. Apart from a review of existing literature, empirical evidence is also explored from a study by Oosthuizen (2016) in order to determine the dimensions of occupational stress (Chapter 3), to explore the relationship between occupational stress and work locus of control (Chapters 6 and 7). It was found that individuals with a strong internal work locus of control are more prone to experience occupational stress. However, it was found that managers with an internal work locus of control tend to cope better with the inherent stressors associated with their roles and that younger managers experience higher levels of occupational stress as opposed to their more experienced counterparts. The practical implications of this book are to enable organisations to retain their key staff that is their managerial employees, by better understanding the factors that influence the manner in which these key individuals perceive and react to occupational stress as determined by their work locus of control orientation. In addition, this book is aimed at educating organisations on the importance of having a sound comprehension of their managers' work locus of control orientation as it is directly linked to job satisfaction and performance. By enhancing these aspects, organisations would enhance their bottom-line as they would have a more productive and motivated managerial team at the helm of their enterprises.

Contents

Abbreviations and Symbols

ANOVA	Analysis of Variance
BEE	Black Economic Empowerment
GDP	Gross Domestic Product
I-E	Internal-External
LOC	Locus of Control
MANOVA	Multivariate Analysis of Variance
SPSS	Statistical Package for the Social Sciences
WLCS	Work Locus of Control Scale
WLOC	Work Locus of Control
WLQ	Work-and-Life Experiences Questionnaire

Chapter 1
Introduction and Background of Occupational Stress and Work Locus of Control

Abstract In this chapter, an overview pertaining to the current state of organisations in South Africa, and how it may influence occupational stress and work locus of control of managers in the local as well as the global context is outlined.

Keywords Depression · Burnout · Globalisation · Diversity · Psychological wellbeing

1.1 Introduction

This book approaches the field of occupational stress from the perspective of South African managers. It explores the consequences of combining current trends and models with supplementary participatory and transformative methods. Unlike past studies, which only focused on obtaining the positivist paradigm to obtain information from participants, our approach is from a positivist approach which explores the experiences of managers related to their Work Locus of Control and their responses are further probed through an interpretivist paradigm to elicit deeper understandings of their occupational stress as it relates to their Work Locus of Control. The book therefore brings a more collective, qualitative, quantitative and transformative approach to occupational stress as it moves beyond a quantitative approach of using surveys only and includes a qualitative angle to data collection such as interviews. Previous research related to the study of the construct of Locus of Control focused on Rotter's ipsative scale, where participants were forced to choose between two options. The Work Locus of Control scale on the other hand is a Likert scale which enables participants to vary their choices. In this way the results obtained have variation and it is easier to gauge how strongly or poorly participants feel about a certain variable. Minimal research has been conducted in industry using the Work Locus of Control scale as most research has used the Locus of Control scale. Finally, most studies have focused on researching the locus of control and occupational stress of nurses and lower level employees. This book focuses on higher level employees, namely managers. The book therefore enhances an understanding of managers' Work locus of Control and their occupational stress which is an understudied phenomenon.

N. MH. Carrim et al., *Occupational Stress in South African Work Culture*, SpringerBriefs in Psychology, https://doi.org/10.1007/978-981-33-6397-7_1

Among all the different life situations, work stands out as an important contributor to stress as most of our time is spent on work, at the place of work or working remotely from home (Adenuga, 2015). Even before the Covid-19 crisis, the modern workplace differed tremendously from the work environment 30–40 years ago (Carrim & Dresselhaus, 2019). COVID-19 crisis brings forth even more attention to occupational stress since work and life merged where most employees work from home, in between home schooling children, and concerns about the global impact of COVID-19 on the economy. Working hours are longer and restructured, it has an impact on organisational cultures and structures as well as a loss of lifetime career paths (Fotinatos-Ventouratos & Cooper, 2005), which leads to heightened stress levels. Branham (2005) stated that one quarter to a half of all individuals employed experience some form of occupational stress, which has dire consequences for employees, which may be heightened during the global crisis. Even before the COVID-19 crisis, Jahanzeb (2010) and Malik, Björkqvist, and Österman (2017) stated that the workplace has become the basis of high levels of stress because of mass retrenchments, demand for greater productivity, technological changes, information overload, an uncertain future and intense competition. In order to keep on par with the competition, workers in organisations spend a large amount of their time endeavouring to meet their job demands, thus ignoring the stressors in the work environment that have a negative effect on their personal, home and social lives, which are more entwined now. Demands of work have a harmful effect on employees both physically and mentally.

Since the workplace is evidently one of the greatest causes of stress, business executives and managers have a responsibility to recognise and aptly manage occupational stress, because an unmanaged stress work environment may have serious consequences for organisations to reach their organisational objectives. Carr, Kelley, Keaton, and Albrecht (2011) found that a relationship exists between stress and poor health. In a South African study, more than 40% of all work-related illness is due to work-related stress, depression and burnout, costing South Africa billions of rands (ANA, 2018). It is estimated that in the United Kingdom occupational stress is responsible for over six million days of sick leave per year, with reasons being related to minor and major illnesses (Ashong, Rogers, Botwe, & Anim-Sampong, 2016).

Within the context of the workplace, in the twenty-first century employee turnover has emerged as an important issue for organisations as they face tight competitive labour markets and skills shortages. It is argued that highly skilled staff such as technical, professional, and most importantly managerial staff are difficult to replace because of their skills and knowledge (Dhir, 2019). While stress may be offset by a sudden unforeseen pressure, it is usually as a result of a combination of stressful factors which accrue over time and cannot be attributed to a single cause of stress. It is therefore imperative to examine the quality of work life for employees in a particular work environment as workplaces vary vastly in specific environments (Ashong et al., 2016).

The levels of stress perceived by individuals in the workplace and the degree to which adverse effects, i.e. psychological and other constraints, conspire to affect them, is largely dependent on the individual's ability to effectively cope with occupational stress (Bhagat et al., 2001). Although research on occupational stress has grown quite significantly in the last 50 years (Ashong et al., 2016; Beehr & Newman, 1978; Bhagat & Beehr, 1985; Cooper & Payne, 1978; Dhir, 2019; Schuler, 1980), research on the effect that an individual's work locus of control (WLOC) has on perceived levels of occupational stress is still rather limited.

Narahari and Koneru (2017) point out that the study of occupational stress in the workplace is important for several reasons: Firstly, stress has harmful physiological and psychological effects on employees. Secondly, stress is a major contributor to employee turnover and absenteeism. Thirdly, when one employee experiences stress, it can cause harm to other employees as well (Narahari & Koneru, 2017). By controlling stress that has dire consequences can result in employees and the organisation being managed more effectively (Carrim, 2012). Occupational stress negatively impacts the performance of employees in the workplace. In most cases occupational stress is a direct result of the job that employees are engaged in (Jayashree, 2010). In most cases employees are not even aware that their occupations are causing stress and subsequently leading to migraine headaches, heart attacks and in extreme cases leading to suicide (Yahaya, Yahaya, Tamyes, Ismael, & Jaalam, 2010). Moreover, the COVID-19 lockdown has added to managers' stress levels as work has to be conducted remotely and brings with it added challenges, namely, upskilling employees to work online, added job responsibilities, an increased number of meetings at odd hours, an increased workload. This book is therefore relevant to this topic as it addresses and highlights how work locus of control orientation enables employees to better cope with their job as well as their work environmental stressors. The objective of the book is to provide an understanding of whether managers with an internal or external locus of work locus of control are able to cope better with workplace stressors.

The arguments made already paint a dim picture of occupational stress and work locus of control in the current workforce and may even be more dire because of economic impact on organisations because of the COVID-19 crisis. Therefore, it is important to understand the workforce and the workplace of today in order to have an informed idea of the origin of occupational stress, and how work locus of control can assist managers to adapt to a changing world of work.

1.2 Management in the Global Context

According to Hellriegeld, Jackson, and Slocum (1999, p. 7), a manager can be defined as "a person who allocates human, material and information resources in pursuit of an organisation's goals." Inherently, the main goal of any organisation, regardless of industry or size, is success-driven. Hence, managers have the responsibility of steering their organisations towards success. According to Martiz (2002), organisational success can be measured twofold. Firstly, in order to survive organisations must be profitable. The very essence of an organisation's' survival lies in sustainable profitability. Secondly, organisational success can be measured on the human level, i.e. employee well-being.

Managers of today are confronted with globalisation and diversity of the workforce. Most countries have a rich cultural diversity and most countries experience the dire effects of economic instability. The biggest challenges are with developing countries where emigration of citizens are more predominant and common than in first world countries (Maritz, 2002). The unique dynamics characteristics of the global workforce (especially in developing countries) force managers to adopt a more proactive approach to management rather to continue with reactive management (Maritz, 2002).

Managers in the new millennium have the daunting task of managing the unique challenges of a diverse workforce in such a manner to steer the economy in the direction of prosperity. According to Maritz (2002), the most significant issues that managers are faced with include globalisation and technology. In developing countries unemployment, and ill-health (physical and psychological) are more prominent than in first world countries.

Against the backdrop of the innate challenges that managers are faced with daily, they also find themselves constantly battling to find a middle course between being competitive in the international market and simultaneously promoting skills development programmes to combat illiteracy. Subsequently, unemployment is a direct result of a skills shortage within developing countries. According to the Management Index Report 2014/2015, recent research indicates more than ever the need for nurturing employee well-being. According to Jeffrey, Mahoney, Michaelson, and Abdullah (2014), psychological well-being and effective coping mechanisms are directly linked to increased levels of job performance, productivity and employee engagement. According to the Management Index Report 2014/2015, 66.63% of managers are of the opinion that their organisations care about their well-being. On the other hand, 59% of managers feel that their organisations would take advantage of them should the opportunity present itself. Furthermore, it has been found that the well-being of managers is promoted by being able to be authentic at work. In a study by Steyn and Bell (2015), it was found that the minority of managers are able to express their authenticity in their immediate work environment, whilst most managers indicated that they are not able to express themselves freely in the work situation.

It is clear that managers have to make a concerted effort to change their managerial approaches to be able to effectively cope with the increasing demands of the country. Managers must increasingly become aware of the realities that they face and accordingly turn the tables by changing these challenges into potential growth opportunities for their respective organisations and South Africa as a whole.

1.3 Importance of Occupational Stress and Work Locus of Control for Managers

Occupational stress appears to be a significant area of interest in management studies since occupational stress can have an extensive impact on individuals' health and safety, which in turn can be directly linked to organisational effectiveness (Van Niekerk, 2011). There are a variety of stressors both internal and external to organisations, as well as the individual's orientation towards WLOC, which have an impact on that person's apparent level of stress. These elements will be addressed in subsequent chapters where firstly, the relationship between an individual's WLOC orientation and apparent levels of occupational stress will be explored. Secondly, the extent of an individual's WLOC orientation and other stressors, inside and outside of the organisation, which might influence the individual, for example demographics and managerial level will also be explored.

Currently, South Africa is facing a major unemployment crisis. There are more entrants in the job market and fewer jobs that are created in the economy. Since the demise of apartheid, profit shares of national income has increased over wage shares. The main reason for the high unemployment rate is the high wages, especially of managers and strict labour laws (Carrim & Senne, 2016, 2019). South Africa is not only in a political-economic transition from apartheid to democracy, but also increasing its economic growth and competitiveness in a global market (Horwitz, 2012). Skills development is fundamental to both these dual imperatives. Moreover, South Africa is an emergent economy that is experiencing high levels of unrest and difficulty and is undergoing transformation from a centralized command and control political economy to a market-oriented economy with varying amounts of state direction (Horwitz, 2012). With an abundance of people who can do manual, unskilled work, but with too few people who have the required technological, managerial and financial skills to occupy positions needing these abilities, South Africa is facing a skills shortage (Carrim & Senne, 2016, 2019). In fact, some MNCs ascribe the difficulties related to the human resource development of black people to these shortages (Quelch & Austin, 2012). Labor legislation, such as the Skills Development Act, 1998 (Act 97 of 1998) and the Employment Equity Act, 1998 (Act 55 of 1998), introduced in the post-apartheid era, aimed to reverse this process by emphasizing human resource development and introducing levy and grant incentives (Horwitz, Browning, Jain, & Steenkamp, 2002). However, skills shortages still plague South Africa, and HR practitioners from overseas parent companies direct investment away from this country as the challenge is that knowledge transfer cannot take place (Wöcke, Bendixen, & Rijamampianina, 2007), resulting in the slow inflow of foreign direct investment (FDI) into the country (Gilroy, Gries, & Naudé, 2006).

Several other challenges faced by managers have been identified in the South African context. One obstacle South African managers face is the retention of Black staff. Booysen (2007) identifies several reasons for the attrition rates of Black employees. First, slow progress of Blacks into management. Second, there is a lack of commitment from managers in the top echelons of organizations enforcing employment equity measures. Third, a white male-dominated culture that excludes Black recruits. Fourth, Blacks are regarded as tokens and not provided responsibility and decision-making power due to stereotypes. Fifth, Black staff are not trained and lack mentors. Sixth, language barriers exist where the majority of employees do not communicate in English. Seventh, HIV and Aids, which have the potential to eradicate the potential gains made through skills development efforts as between 15 and 20% of the population is infected with the virus. These barriers result in many MNCs not willing to enter a host country (Du Plessis & Huntley, 2009).

Subsequent chapters will determine to what extent WLOC has an impact on managers' perceptions of occupational stress. By formulating a scientifically based understanding of the relationship between the two constructs, the researcher aims to empower South African managers to more effectively manage their occupational stress by understanding how their WLOC directly influences their levels of stress. Accordingly, by empowering managers to conceptualise the source of their occupational stress, the ultimate aim is to assist managers in the management of their environment according to their WLOC orientation and thereby decrease their stress levels at work.

1.4 Contribution of This Study to the Field of Human Resource Management

The aim of this book is to provide organisations with a tool to effectively manage the impact that fluctuations in any economy can have on organisations. Therefore, an investigation of the relationship and dynamics between occupational stress and WLOC orientation amongst managers in the South African workplace which has experienced major fluctuations serves as one example that managers globally can tap into. This book will provide a greater in-depth perspective into occupational stress by identifying stressors, inside and outside of the organisation, that cause the highest levels of stress.

From a theoretical perspective, the book will make three valuable contributions to the extant body of knowledge on the relationship between occupational stress and WLOC. Firstly, the book highlights an under-explored area between occupational stress and managers' orientation towards WLOC. The book highlights which stressors cause the highest levels of stress among South African management.

From a practical perspective, because of recent fluctuations in various economies, the South African economy being one of them, the book will assist organisations to identify and accordingly manage occupational stressors to control the effects they may have on managers' ability to function at an optimal level.

1.5 Outline of Subsequent Chapters

Subsequent chapters will consist of the following:

- Chapter 2: Occupational stress amongst managers
- Chapter 3: Causes of Occupational stress
- Chapter 4: Consequences of occupational stress
- Chapter 5: Work locus of control amongst managers
- Chapter 6: The relationship between occupational stress and work locus of control
- Chapter 7: Conclusion, practical implications and recommendations

Summary of Chapter 1

The premise of this chapter was to introduce and orientate the concepts of occupational stress and work locus of control to the reader. The impact of these variables on effective management and organisational outcomes were explored. When not handled, the costs to the organisation are great pertaining to employee turnover, absenteeism, and overall productivity of employees and the organisation. As the world of work are changing, causes and outcomes of occupational stress and the extend thereof should be monitored and managers need to be conscious of the effect it has on the work locus of control their employees. This will be further discussed in the following chapters.

References

Adenuga, O. A. (2015). Impact of occupational stress on job satisfaction and mental health of first bank employees: Implication for personnel psychologists. *Science, 1*(1), 15–21.

African News Agency (ANA). (2018, April 24). *Work-related sickness costs SA billions of rands.* Retrieved from https://citizen.co.za/news/south-africa/1905408/work-related-sickness-costs-sa-billions-of-rands/.

Ashong, G. G. N. A., Rogers, H., Botwe, B. O., & Anim-Sampong, S. (2016). Effects of occupational stress and coping mechanisms adopted by radiographers in Ghana. *Radiography, 22*(2), 112–117.

Beehr, T. A., & Newman, J. E. (1978). Job stress, employee health, and organizational effectiveness: A facet analysis, model, and literature review. *Personnel Psychology, 31,* 665–699.

Bhagat, R. S., & Beehr, T. A. (1985). An evaluation summary and recommendations for future research. In T. A. Beehr & R. S. Bhagat (Eds.), *Human stress and cognition in organization: An integrated perspective.* New York: John Wiley.

Bhagat, R. S., Ford, D. L., O'Driscoll, M. P., Frey, L., Babakus, E., & Mahanyele, M. (2001). Do South African managers cope differently from American managers? A cross-cultural investigation. *International Journal of Intercultural Relations, 25,* 301–313.

Booysen, L. (2007). Barriers to employment equity implementation and retention of blacks in management in South Africa. *South African Journal of Labour Relations, 31*(1), 47–71.

Branham, L. (2005). Planning to become an employer of choice. *Journal of Organizational Excellence, 24*(3), 57–68.

Carr, J., Kelley, B., Keaton, R., & Albrecht, C. (2011). Getting to grips with stress in the workplace: Strategies for promoting a healthier, more productive environment. *Human Resource Management International Digest, 19*(4), 32–38.

Carrim, N. M. H. (2012). The relationship amongst locus of control, self-determination and job satisfaction in call centres. Unpublished master's thesis, University of Pretoria, Pretoria, South Africa.

Carrim, N. M. H., & Dresselhaus, F. (2019). Vicarious education, dialogue education and self-efficacy among Indian female students in a diversity management course. *Africa Education Review, 16*(5), 29–46.

Carrim, N. M. H., & Senne, Y. (2016). Challenges faced by South African human resource practitioners in multinational companies. In N. Zakaria, I. Abdul-Talib, & N. Osman (Eds.), *Handbook of research on impacts of international business and political affairs on the global economy* (pp. 133–153). Hershey, PA, USA: IGI Global Publishers.

Carrim, N. M. H., & Senne, Y. (2019). Life context model, intersectionality, and black feminist epistemology: Women managers in Africa. In E. T. Pereira & P. Paoloni (Eds.), *Handbook of research on women in management and the global labor market* (pp. 136–155). Hershey, PA, USA: IGI Global Publishers.

Cooper, C. L., & Payne, R. (1978). *Stress at work.* Chichester: John Wiley.

Dhir, S. (2019). *The changing nature of work, leadership, and organizational culture in future ready organizations.* Published senior thesis. Retrieved from https://scholarship.claremont.edu/cgi/viewcontent.cgi?article=3092&context=cmc_theses.

Du Plessis, A. J., & Huntley, K. (2009). Challenges in a globalised context for international human resource managers in South African organisations. *International Review of Business Research Papers, 5*(1), 413–427.

Fotinatos-Ventouratos, R., & Cooper, C. (2005). The role of gender and social class in work stress. *Journal of Managerial Psychology, 20*(1), 14–23.

Gilroy, B. M., Gries, T., & Naudé, W. A. (2006). *Multinational enterprises, foreign direct investment and growth in Africa: South African perspectives.* Dordrecht, Netherlands: Springer Science & Business Media.

Hellriegel, D., Jackson, S. E., & Slocum, J. W. (1999). *Management.* Cincinnati, OH: South-Western.

Horwitz, F. M. (2012). Evolving human resource management in Southern African multinational firms: towards an Afro-Asian nexus. *The International Journal of Human Resource Management, 23*(14), 2938–2958.

Horwitz, F. M., Browning, V., Jain, H., & Steenkamp, A. J. (2002). Human resource practices and discrimination in South Africa: Overcoming the apartheid legacy. *International Journal of Human Resource Management, 13*(7), 1105–1118.

Jahanzeb, H. (2010). The impact of job stress on job satisfaction among academic faculty of a mega distance learning institution in Pakistan: A case study of Allama Iqbal open university. *Mustang Journal of Business and Ethics, 1,* 31–48.

Jayashree, R. (2010). Stress management with special reference to public sector bank employees in Chennai. *International Journal of Enterprise and Innovation Management Studies, 1*(3), 34–35.

Jeffrey, K., Mahoney, S., Michaelson, J., & Abdullah, S. (2014). *Well-being at work: A review of the literature.* New Economics Foundation. Retrieved June 5, 2016, from http://www.neweconomics.org/issues/entry/well-being.

Malik, A., Björkqvist, K., & Österman, K. (2017). Factors associated with occupational stress among University Teachers in Pakistan and Finland. *Journal of Educational, Health and Community Psychology, 6*(2), 1–14.

Martiz, T. (2002). A comparison between the June 1991 and Series 2000 JBCC Preliminaries editions. *Acta Structilia, 9*(1), 79–93.

Narahari, C. L., & Koneru, D. K. (2017). A study on the role of occupational stress in organisations. *International Journal of Engineering Techology, Engineering, Management and Applied Science, 5,* 53–59.

Quelch, J. A., & Austin, J. E. (2012). Should multinationals invest in Africa? *Image,* 1–8.

Schuler, R. S. (1980, April). Definition and conceptualization of stress in organizations. In *Organizational behavior and human performance* (p. 189). Adapted from Robbins (2005).

Steyn, C., & Bell, D. (2015). *Management Index Report 2014/ 2015*. Retrieved June 5, 2016, from http://www.usb-ed.com/ManagementIndexReport/MIR2015.pdf.

Van Niekerk, M. (2011). The relationship between occupational stress and locus of control among nurses. Unpublished master's dissertation, University of Pretoria, Pretoria, South Africa.

Wöcke, A., Bendixen, M., & Rijamampianina, R. (2007). Building flexibility into multi-national human resource strategy: A study of four South African multinational enterprises. *International Journal of Human Resource Management, 18*(5), 829–844.

Yahaya, N., Yahaya, A., Tamyes, F. A., Ismail, J., & Jaalam, S. (2010). The Effect of various modes of occupational stress, job satisfaction, intention to leave and absenteeism companies commission of Malaysia. *Australian Journal of Basic and Applied Sciences, 4*(7), 1676–1684.

Chapter 2
Occupational Stress Among Managers

Abstract This chapter provides various definitions of stress and occupational stress. The definition of work locus of control is also provided. The theoretical underpinning namely, the Transactional approach and the Job Demands Control Support model are also discussed. The chapter also outlines the types of stress encountered as well as the outcomes of stress.

Keywords Epidemiology of occupational stress · Psychological strain · Person-environment fit model · Transactional approach · Job demands control support model

2.1 Origin and Conceptualisation of Occupational Stress

In the twenty-first century stress is an inevitable part of life for most individuals and can be even more heightened because of the COVID-19 crisis. Stress from work can be caused by a variety of factors that might be internal or external to an individual's work circumstances. According to Cooper and Cartwright (1994), one of the first scientific attempts and most well-known definitions of stress was constructed by Hans Seyle in 1946. Cooper and Cartwright (1994, p. 8) state that Seyle defined stress as "the non-specific response of the body to any demand created upon it. The demand can be a threat, a challenge or any kind of change which requires the body to adapt or mobilise energy". Ridner (2004, p. 537) states that in modern literature stress can be defined as "a constraining force, influence of a force exerted when one body part pushes against another; emphasis, intense effort, or the predominance of a sound inverse". Furthermore, Ridner (2004, p. 537) notes that stress as a transitive verb can be defined as being subject to psychological or physical stress.

Occupational stress (also known as job stress), on the other hand refers to the inability to cope with the pressures in a job, due to a poor fit between an employee's abilities and the individual's work requirements and conditions (Holmlund-Rytkönen & Strandvik, 2005; Malik, Björkqvist, & Österman, 2017). Occupational stress is not an objective but rather a subjective phenomenon which includes the employee's active interpretation of his or her objective circumstances. Potential stressors are not fundamentally negative or severe. However, individual differences in coping style

N. MH. Carrim et al., *Occupational Stress in South African Work Culture*,
SpringerBriefs in Psychology, https://doi.org/10.1007/978-981-33-6397-7_2

and cognitive appraisal allow for the same stressor to be experienced by some as a challenge and by others as a hindrance (Hendel & Horn, 2008). Hence, occupational stress becomes a condition where employees feel under threat and unwelcome. Occupational stress should therefore not only be regarded as a problem of the individual, but as a serious problem in the organisation.

Other definitions of occupational stress also exist. Occupational stress is also defined as any force that strains a physical or psychological factor beyond its range of ability, which then subsequently produces strain within an individual (Arnold, Cooper, & Robinson, 1995). Although it is noted that numerous definitions of stress may be found in the literature, Monat and Lazarus (1991) argue that there is no coherence on any specific definition on stress between stress researchers and academics. Since stress can be defined in several different ways (Nelson & Burke, 2000), stress in this book subscribes to Lazarus and Folkman (1984) and Hancock and Desmond's (2001) two key insights into stress: (i) that is, that stress should be studied and understood through a multidimensional perspective, and (ii) stress should be viewed as a dynamic phenomenon. Furthermore, the following definition is also applicable in this book where Storm Pallesen (2007, p. 8), defined stress as "an environmental condition and a form of response to it". Furthermore, stress can be conceptualised as the relationship perceived between environmental demands and an individual's abilities to meet these environmental demands (Storm Pallesen, 2007). Muhonen and Torkelson (2004) as well as Schreuder and Coetzee (2008, p. 277) state that stress in this regard can be explained as situations where individuals experience those environmental demands that exceed their capacity to deal with these demands.

Occupational stress is defined by Kyriacou (2001) as one experiencing negative emotional states such as worry, depression, frustration and anxiety. Topper (2007) regards occupational stress can also be defined as the view that there is a discrepancy between the environmental demands (stressors) and individual capacities to realise these demands.

Quick and Henderson (2016) regard occupational stress as a risk factor that requires major reflection on the life history of the situation. According to these authors occupational stress is not a toxic or an acute condition that can be cured through the means of treatment. Rather, it is a chronic condition that needs to be understood in terms of its epidemiology and/or life history of the situation and/or problem before exploring prevention, protection and intervention alternatives. According to Quick and Henderson (2016), the epidemiology of occupational stress can be viewed in three stages. The first stage deals with causes of stress which are viewed as risk factors. The second stage is the stress response which is a normal and naturally occurring reaction to internal pressures and environmental demands. The third stage includes the consequences of the life history, which include either forms of eustress which is healthy stress or forms of distress which include psychological, medical and behavioural elements. In addition to the main stem of the life history of occupational stress, the stress response displays many individual difference modifiers which may either make the employee more vulnerable or serve as protection factors for the employee. Since occupational stress is not a specific disorder, it tends to attack a weak point, which is the Archille's heel of the employee. This is also referred to as the Weak Organ hypothesis. Cooper and Payne (1978) also focused on the epidemiology of work stress for blue-collar and white-collar workers and the family being the cause of adding to occupational stress. Distress is a third factor that is caused due to intense, prolonged and frequent exposure to stress. Distress can occur in three forms, namely, psychological, medical or behavioural. Medical distress manifests in terms of cancers, heart diseases and musculoskeletal injuries with their related disability and pain. Occupational stress has been identified as a major element in cardiovascular disease. Landsbergis et al. (2011) linked cardiovascular disease to conditions at work such as shift work, social isolation and physical hazards. Baum, Trevino, and Dougall (2011) indicate that cancers are caused by occupational stress and having an indirect role in worsening the disease and limiting recovery.

Occupational stress has been recognised as a major health issue for organisations both in the short and long term, given that it leads to issues at work such as negative emotional reactions, physical health problems and counterproductive behaviour (Spector, 2002). In studies pertaining to occupational stress, it has been noted that an increasing interest in the role of generalised LOC has emerged, but that only a few studies (Blau, 1993; Orpen, 1992) have utilised the WLOC measure.

Yahaya, Yahaya, Tamyes, Ismail, and Jaalam (2010) identified five sources of stress in the workplace. The first source of stress is intrinsic to the job and include factors such as time pressures, work overload and poor physical working conditions. The second source manifests due to the role of the employee in the organisation which includes role conflict and role ambiguity. The third source of occupational stress is due to career development which includes over/under promotion as well as lack of job security. Relationships at work which include poor relations with colleagues or supervisors an extreme example being workplace bullying, is the fourth source of stress. The fifth source of stress stems from the organisational climate and structure of the organisation and includes minimal involvement in decision-making and high levels of office politics (Beheshtifar, Mohammad-Rafiei, & Nekoie-Moghadam, 2013).

Botha and Pienaar (2006) on the other hand maintain that the causes of occupational stress stem from sitting for long periods of time, perceived loss of job, and security, lack of safety, lifting heavy objects, lack of autonomy in one's job and repetitiveness. The authors also contend that occupational stress is caused by a lack of equipment and resources; erratic work schedules (for example, working overtime or on late shifts) and organizational climate are considered as contributors to employees stress. Branham (2005) asserts that occupational stress is caused by many factors including when workplaces will not or cannot supply equipment necessary for their workforce to work efficiently and produce their jobs.

2.2 Theory Relevant to Occupational Stress: Transactional Approach

On the basis of the previous discussion, Hart (1994) suggest that theories should embrace a transactional approach to stress. A transactional approach suggests that stress should be treated as a dynamic process functioning between an individual and his or her environment (Hart & Cooper, 2001). Multiple authors maintain that the term "transaction" is used to accentuate the fact that stress is perceived as the result of the aggregation between personal and environmental variables (Cox, 1978; Hart & Cooper, 2001; Lazarus & Folkman, 1984). In this regard, Hart and Cooper (2001) argue that transactional models are characterised by this dynamic, reciprocal nature of the relationship between personal and environmental variables.

The stressors and strain approach is based on the assumption that stressors cause strain, allowing no sanction for the fact that a reciprocal causal relationship may exist between stressors and strain. Thus, in the light of the transactional approach to stress, it can be noted that even though the stressors and strain approach is deemed to be the dominant theme in occupational stress literature, the need for a more dynamic and reciprocal theory is evident.

The transactional approach has given way to the development of specific occupational stress theories, such as the person-environment fit model (Hart & Cooper, 2001). The person-environment fit model suggests that a misfit exists between the characteristics of an individual and his or her work environment, and that this misfit will subsequently result in physiological, psychological and behavioural strain (Hart & Cooper, 2001). Van Niekerk (2011) contends that the person-environment fit can be theorised as "the fit between person and the environment [that] determines the amount of stress a person perceives" (Landy & Conte, 2007, p. 436); or as the "amount of strain experienced by an individual [that] is proportional to the degree of misfit between the person and the environment" (Fogarty & Machin, 2003, p. 4).

According to Ganster and Schaubroeck (1991), the basic principle of the person-environment theory is that the stressfulness that is experienced by the individual can be attributed to the degree of fit between the individual and the job environment. On these premises, two types of fit are generally specified: "(a) that between outcomes provided by the job and the needs, motives, or preferences of the individual, and (b) that between the demands and requirements of the job and the skills and abilities of the worker" (Ganster & Schaubroeck, 1991, p. 240). Ivancevich, Konopasle, and DeFrank (2003) argue that the two types of fit, as described by Ganster and Schaubroeck (1991), can be seen as a demands-abilities fit. According to Van Niekerk (2011), demands can be seen as the individual's duties and expectations in regard to his or her job role, whereas abilities can be viewed as an individual's competencies, knowledge and skills. Therefore, in regard the person-environment fit model, when the individual's contributions meet the environmental demands a state of demands-abilities fit is achieved.

Furthermore, it is noted that the supplies in the person-environment fit model encompass resources such as training opportunities, supervisor's recognition and the availability of resources. In this regard, it can be concluded that when the environment satisfies the individual's needs, desires and preferences the needs-supplies fit is achieved (Sekiguchi, 2004). Furthermore, Sekiguchi states that in order for the person-environment fit model to achieve a state of supplies and demands fit, both the individual and the environment need to refer to the same facet. From this statement, stress is viewed as something that individuals experience in "situations where they perceive that the demands in the environment exceed their capacity to deal with them" (Muhonen & Torkelson, 2004). On the contrary, a good person-environment fit in the work context exists when an individual's expertise and abilities match the requirements of the position and work conditions (Landy & Conte, 2007).

An objective and subjective representation exists between the individual and the environment (Harrison in Ivancevich et al., 2003). The objective individual exerts his or her characteristics in actual terms, such as stating that he or she is technically skilled with six years of experience (Ivancevich et al., 2003). Whereas, the subjective individual will refer to his or her perception of personal attributes, such as self-efficacy (Webster, 2006) and values (LaDou, 2007).

Furthermore, it can also be seen that the objective and subjective environment also has an impact on the person-environment fit. According to the theory, the objective environment is regarded as the actual work environment of individuals, whereas the subjective environment is regarded to be the individual's awareness of his or her physical and social work conditions (Ivancevich et al., 2003). It is imperative to recognise the importance of both the person and the environment in order to understand the nature and consequences of stress, seeing that in turn stress affects behaviours, attitudes and the overall well-being of employees (Spies, 2004). Commitment (including the individual's commitment to the organization and the organization's commitment to the individual) refers to an effect of stress. Poor health is an outcome of stress, which can be used to ascertain if workplace pressures have positive and motivating or negative and damaging effects. However, poor health may not necessarily be indicative of workplace stress. Individuals may, for example, be unwell because they choose not to lead a healthy lifestyle or may be unaware of how to do so (Jackson & Rothmann, 2006).

2.3 Models Relevant to Occupational Stress

Karasek (1979) advocated for the Job Demands Control Support (JDCS) Model as a model for occupational stress. This model includes two aspects in work context, namely, job control and job demand. Job demand includes psychological stressors, such as the quantity and difficulty of tasks as well as short work time. Job control (or job decision latitude) on the other hand focuses on two dimensions, namely, decision authority and skill discretion. The Social Support dimension was also added to the JDC Model and named it the Job Demand-Control-Support Model (Narahari & Koneru, 2017). In the JDCS model psychological strain (anxiety, fatigue and depression) and ill health are perceived as potential consequences of highly demanding jobs, low social support and low job control at work from colleagues and/or the supervisor (Adriaenssens, De Gucht, & Maes, 2015). The JDCS model explains a vital part of the variance in stress-health outcomes. Other factors such as organisational characteristics have increased the prediction of wellbeing and health outcomes (Pisanti, van der Doef, Maes, Lazzari, & Bertini, 2011). In terms of this model lack of skill discretion and decision authority are related to occupational stress (Adriaenssens, De Gucht, Van Der Doef, & Maes, 2011). A lack of support from peers and supervisors strongly predicts psychosomatic distress in nurses (Adriaenssens et al., 2011).

Narahari and Koneru (2017) assert that in 1997, Robbins developed the Stress Effect Model. In terms of this model individual and organisational stressors can be organised into five categories: First, organisational practices which include supervisory practices, performance reward systems and promotional opportunities. Second, task/job features which include autonomy and workload. Third, organisational climate and culture which includes integrity, personal growth and employee value. Fourth, interpersonal relationships with customers, peers and supervisors. Fifth, the employee's personal characteristics such as family relationships, personality traits and coping skills (Narahari & Koneru, 2017).

Narahari and Koneru (2017) posit that Cartwright and Cooper (2002) proposed a model which embraces occupational strain (ill-health), stressors and organisational commitment. The authors identified seven occupational stressors. The first occupational stressor is work relationships which includes unsupportive or poor relations with supervisors, peers as well as unfair treatment and isolation. The second occupational stressor is work-life imbalance which focuses on when work interferes with an employee's home life and personal life. The third occupational stressor is overload and refers to extraordinary time pressures and unmanageable workloads. The fourth occupational stressor is job security which includes obsolescence and fear of losing one's job. The fifth occupational stressor is control which in this case refers to a lack of influence in the way work is performed and organised. The sixth occupational stressor is resources and communication which refers to having the proper resources, equipment and training. The seventh occupational stressor is pay and benefit which includes the financial rewards associated with work and the elements of the job, referring to the fundamental nature of the job itself which can be a source of stress (Narahari & Koneru, 2017).

Narahari and Koneru (2017) point out that Burke (1988) clustered job stressors into six categories: role stressors, physical environment, relationships with others, organisational structure and job chracterisitcs, work-family conflict and career development. Narahari and Koneru (2017) further state that Cooper (1988) identified six causes of stress in the workplace: relationships with others, organisational climate and structure, factors intrinsic to the job, work/home interface, management role and achievement and career. Thus, conditions that make jobs stressful can either be exogenous (that is, unfavourable occupational conditions, lack of collaboration, excessive workload etc) or endogenous pressures (that is, individual personality characteristics, etc) (Narahari & Koneru, 2017).

2.4 Types of Occupational Stressors

Over the past decade research on work-related stress and strain has increased significantly (see De Simone, Cicotto, & Lampis, 2016; Malik et al., 2017). The increasing amount of research on occupational stress has highlighted many of the associated costs and personal consequences that excessive stress in the workplace may have (Malik et al., 2017). Furthermore, it is noted that the effects of occupational stress can have dire effects for both the individual and organisations (De Simone et al., 2016). In this regard, Adriaenssens, Hamelink, and Van Bogaert (2017) maintained that excessive occupational demands can lead to anxiety, job dissatisfaction, depression, and in severe cases can even cause mental and physical disabilities right through to coronary heart disease. A number of stressors in the work environment can cause individuals to perceive overwhelming levels of stress. The most common stressors, as identified by Markow and Pieters (2012), are work relationships, overload, job security, aspects of the job, work-life balance, control, pay and benefits, resources and communication.

2.5 Outcomes of Occupational Stress

In organisational research, occupational stress has been recognised to be a major concern for employees, because it tends to have an adverse impact on both the physiological and psychological health of the individual (Greenhaus, Callanan, & Godshalh, 2000). Thus, occupational stress can evidently result in negative consequences, such as job dissatisfaction, burnout, depression and psychosomatic illness (Greenhaus et al., 2000). Moreover, high levels of stress can also lead to feelings of anxiety, anger, irritability, tension, nervousness and boredom (Pieters, 2011). According to Schreuder and Coetzee (2008), these feelings experienced by individuals may in turn lead to lower job-performance, resentment of supervision, decreased self-esteem, worker conflict and an inability to concentrate and make decisions. Due to the apprehensive impact that occupational stress has proven to have on employees, researchers have increasingly become more interested in the role that the generalised control beliefs, also termed LOC, of an individual have in managing this perceived stress.

In a study by Oosthuizen (2016), it was found that managers' do not experience occupational stress based on their gender, race, marital status, total number of dependents, qualification level, management level, number of subordinates, management experiences, and whether they work day or night shifts. Oosthuizen (2016) stated that maybe the reason could be that managers are more informed and make better career choices that are not construed to circumstances or cultural and educational background. Chen and Silversthorne (2008) also found this in a study. Haque and Aston (2016) in a study based on 825 (403 respondents from UK and 422 from Pakistan) employees found on the other hand that female employees are less stressed compared to male workers. The study also found that female managers deal more effectively with occupational stress compared to male managers. The study revealed that managers from Pakistan experienced more stress than UK managers. Jain, Jabeen, Mishra, and Gupta (2007) compared the occupational stress levels of 158 engineers and managers in India and found that engineers experienced a greater level of occupational stress compared to managers. Mohammad Mosadeghrad (2014) in a cross-sectional study of 608 employees in Iran found that organisational factors increase occupational stress. The major sources of occupational stress in the study was found to be inadequate pay, inequality at work, too much work, staff shortage, poor recognition and promotion, time pressure, job insecurity and lack of management support. High levels of occupational stress have been linked to an increased risk of physical injuries, cardiovascular disease, high blood pressure, depression and increases in negative personal behaviours such as anger, anxiety and irritability. Occupational stress was also found to be positively related with employees' turnover intentions. A study by Yahaya et al. (2010) based on results from 100 employees in Malaysia on the other hand found that factors such as the external environment contribute to the occupational stress. The researchers found that occupational stress do not have a direct effect on intention to leave and absenteeism but have direct negative effect on job satisfaction. Job satisfaction was found to have a negative effect on intention to leave and absenteeism.

Oosthuizen (2016), however, did find that a manager's age could influence the level of occupational stress. It was found that younger managers experience greater levels of occupational stress due to the expectations they have of their work environment as compared to their more seasoned counterparts. It may be also because younger managers are still working hard on their career goals, while older managers are more established and have a sounder career outlook than their younger counterparts.

Summary of Chapter 2

This chapter described the concept of occupational stress, and provided insight of its origin and foundation. Occupational stress has been studied for decades, and has major health implications for employees on the short-term and long-term. Occupational stress is based on the reaction of external stimuli from an individual, and the intensity thereof is dependent on the individual's perceived evaluation on the importance of a particular external stimuli. Different stages of occupational stress from various authors were mentioned and elaborated on, and although in this chapter, the causes and consequences of occupational stress were discussed, in the following two chapters, these elements will be debated in more depth.

References

Adriaenssens, J., De Gucht, V., & Maes, S. (2015). Causes and consequences of occupational stress in emergency nurses, a longitudinal study. *Journal of Nursing Management, 23*(3), 346–358.

Adriaenssens, J., De Gucht, V., Van Der Doef, M., & Maes, S. (2011). Exploring the burden of emergency care: Predictors of stress-health outcomes in emergency nurses. *Journal of Advanced Nursing, 67*(6), 1317–1328.

Adriaenssens, J., Hamelink, A., & Van Bogaert, P. (2017). Predictors of occupational stress and well-being in First-Line Nurse Managers: A cross-sectional survey study. *International Journal of Nursing Studies, 73*, 85–92.

Arnold, J., Cooper, C., & Robertson, T. (1995). *Work psychology* (2nd ed.). London, UK: Pitman.

Baum, A., Trevino, L. A., & Dougall, A. L. (2011). Stress and the cancers. In R. J. Contrada & R. J. Baum (Eds.), *The handbook of stress science: Biology, psychology, and health* (pp. 411–424). New York, NY, USA: Springer Publishing Company LLC.

Beheshtifar, M., Mohammad-Rafiei, R., & Nekoie-Moghadam, M. (2013). The investigation of relation between occupational stress and career plateau interdisciplinary. *Journal of Contemporary Research in Business, 4*(11), 650–660.

Blau, G. (1993). Testing the relationship of locus of control to different performance dimensions. *Journal of Occupational and Organizational Psychology, 66*, 125–138.

Botha, C., & Pienaar, J. (2006). South African correctional official occupational stress: The role of psychological strengths. *Journal of Criminal Justice, 34*(1), 73–84.

Branham, L. (2005). Planning to become an employer of choice. *Journal of Organizational Excellence, 24*(3), 57–68.

Burke, R. J. (1988). Some antecedents of work-family conflict. *Journal of Social Behavior and Personality, 3*(4), 287–294.

Cartwright, S., & Cooper, C. L. (2002). *ASSET: An organizational stress screening tool*. London, UK: Robertson Cooper Limited and Cubiks.

Chen, J., & Silversthorne, C. (2008). The impact of locus of control on job stress, job performance and job satisfaction in Taiwan. *Leadership and Organisation Development Journal, 29*(7), 572–582.

Cooper, H. M. (1988). Organizing knowledge syntheses: A taxonomy of literature reviews. *Knowledge in Society, 1*(1), 104.

Cooper, C. L., & Payne, R. (1978). *Stress at work*. Chichester: John Wiley.

Cooper, C. L., & Cartwright, S. (1994). Healthy mind, healthy organisation: A proactive approach to occupational stress. *Human Relations, 47*, 455–470.

Cox, T. (1978). *Stress*. London, UK: Macmillan.

De Simone, S., Cicotto, G., & Lampis, J. (2016). Occupational stress, job satisfaction and physical health in teachers. *Revue Européenne de Psychologie Appliquée, 66*, 65–77.

Fogarty, G. J., & Machin, M. A. (2003). *Discrepancy between preferred and actual levels of exposure to occupational stressors and resulting feelings of strain*. Queensland, Australia: University of Southern Queensland.

Ganster, D. C., & Schaubroeck, J. (1991). Work stress and employee health. *Journal of Management, 17*(2), 235–271.

Greenhaus, J. H., Callanan, G. A., & Godshalh, V. M. (2000). *Career management* (3rd ed.). London, UK: Thomson.

Hancock, P. A., & Desmond, P. A. (2001). *Stress, workload and fatigue*. Mahwah, NJ: Lawrence Erlbaum.

Haque, A. U., & Aston, J. (2016). A relationship between occupational stress and organisational commitment of IT sector's employees in contrasting economies. *Polish Journal of Management Studies, 14*(1), 95–105.

Hart, P. M. (1994). Teacher quality of work life: Integrating work experiences, psychological distress and morale. *Journal of Occupational and Organizational Psychology, 67*, 109–132.

Hart, P. M., & Cooper, C. L. (2001). Occupational stress: Toward a more integrated framework. In N. Anderson, D. S. Ones, H. K. Sinangil, & C. Viswesvaran (Eds.), *Handbook of Industrial, Work and Organizational Psychology* (pp. 93–114). London: Sage Publications.

Hendel, D. D., & Horn, A. S. (2008). The relationship between academic life conditions and perceived sources of faculty stress over time. *Journal of Human Behavior in the Social Environment, 17*(1–2), 61–88.

Holmlund-Rytkönen, M., & Strandvik, T. (2005). Stress in business relationships. *Journal of Business and Industrial Marketing, 20*(1), 12–22.

Ivancevich, J. M., Konopasle, R., & DeFrank, R. S. (2003). Business travel stress: A model, propositions and managerial implications. *Work and Stress, 17*(2), 138–157.

Jackson, L., & Rothmann, S. (2006). Occupational stress, organisational commitment, and ill-health of educators in the North West Province. *South African Journal of Education, 26*(1), 75–95.

Jain, K. K., Jabeen, F., Mishra, V., & Gupta, N. (2007). Job satisfaction as related to organizational climate and occupational stress: A case study of Indian Oil. *International Review of Business Research Papers, 3*(5), 193–208.

Karasek Jr., R. A. (1979). Job demands, job decision latitude, and mental strain: Implications for job redesign. *Administrative Science Quarterly, 24,* 285–308.

Kyriacou, C. (2001). Teacher stress: Directions for future research. *Educational Review, 53*(1), 27–35.

LaDou, J. (2007). *Current occupational and environmental medicine* (4th ed.). New York, NY: McGraw-Hill.

Landsbergis, P. A., Schnall, P. L., Belkic, K. L., Baker, D., Schwartz, J. E., & Pickering, T. G. (2011). Workplace and cardiovascular disease: Relevance and potential role for occupational health psychology. In J. C. Quick & L. E. Tetrick (Eds.), *Handbook of occupational health psychology* (pp. 37–54). Washington, DC, USA: American Psychological Association.

Landy, F. J., & Conte, J. M. (2007). *Work in the 21st century: An introduction to industrial and organisational psychology* (2nd ed.). Danvers, MA: Blackwell.

Lazarus, R. S., & Folkman, S. (1984). *Stress, appraisal, and coping.* New York, NY: Springer.

Malik, A., Björkqvist, K., & Österman, K. (2017). Factors associated with occupational stress among University Teachers in Pakistan and Finland. *Journal of Educational, Health and Community Psychology, 6*(2), 1–14.

Markow, D., & Pieters, A. (2012). *Metlife survey of the American teacher: Teachers, parents, and the economy.* Retrieved August 29, 2014, from www.metlife.com.

Mohammad Mosadeghrad, A. (2014). Occupational stress and its consequences: Implications for health policy and management. *Leadership in Health Services, 27*(3), 224–239.

Monat, A., & Lazarus, R. S. (1991). *Stress and coping. An anthology.* New York, NY: Columbia University Press.

Muhonen, T., & Torkelson, E. (2004). Work locus of control and its relationship to health and job satisfaction from a gender perspective. *Stress and Health, 20,* 21–28.

Narahari, C. L., & Koneru, D. K. (2017). A study on the role of occupational stress in organisations. *International Journal of Engineering Techology, Engineering, Management and Applied Science, 5,* 53–59.

Nelson, D. L., & Burke, R. J. (2000). Women executives: Health, stress, and success. *Academy of Management Perspectives, 14*(2), 107–121.

Oosthuizen, M. M. (2016). *The relationship between occupational stress and Work Locus of Control amongst South African Management: An exploratory study.* Unpublished MCom dissertation, University of Pretoria, Pretoria, South Africa.

Orpen, C. (1992). The work locus of control scale as a predictor of employee attitudes and behaviour: A validity study. *Journal of Human Behavior, 2,* 35–37.

Pieters, W. R. (2011). *The relationship among psychological empowerment, job satisfaction and organisational commitment of staff members at the University of Namibia.* Unpublished PhD dissertation, University of Namibia, Windhoek, Namibia.

Pisanti, R., van der Doef, M., Maes, S., Lazzari, D., & Bertini, M. (2011). Job characteristics, organizational conditions, and distress/well-being among Italian and Dutch nurses: A cross-national comparison. *International Journal of Nursing Studies, 48*(7), 829–837.

Quick, J. C., & Henderson, D. F. (2016). Occupational stress: Preventing suffering, enhancing wellbeing. *International Journal of Environmental Research and Public Health, 13*(5), 459–465.

Ridner, S. H. (2004). Psychological distress: Concept analysis. *Journal of Advanced Nursing, 45*(5), 536–545.

Schreuder, A. M. G., & Coetzee, M. (2008). *Careers: An organisational perspective.* Cape Town, South Africa: Juta.

Sekiguchi, T. (2004). Person-organisation fit and person-job fit in employee selection: A review of the literature. *Osaka Keidai Ronshu, 54*(6), 179–196.

Spector, P. E. (2002). Employee control and occupational stress. *Current Directions in Psychosocial Science, 11*(4), 133–136.

Spies, J. (2004). The relationship between occupational stressors, occupational stress and burnout among trauma unit nursing staff. Unpublished master's dissertation, University of Pretoria, Pretoria, South Africa.

Storm Pallesen, E. (2007). Work-related stress and health and stress among hotel employees in Malmo. Unpublished master's dissertation, Kristianstad University, Kristianstad, Sweden.

Topper, E. F. (2007). Stress in the library. *Journal of New Library, 108*(11/12), 561–564.

Van Niekerk, M. (2011). The relationship between occupational stress and locus of control among nurses. Unpublished master's dissertation, University of Pretoria, Pretoria, South Africa.

Webster, R. E. (2006). *CLEP: Introduction to educational psychology.* Piscataway, NY: Research and Education Association.

Yahaya, N., Yahaya, A., Tamyes, F. A., Ismail, J., & Jaalam, S. (2010). The effect of various modes of occupational stress, job satisfaction, intention to leave and absenteeism companies commission of Malaysia. *Australian Journal of Basic and Applied Sciences, 4*(7), 1676–1684.

Chapter 3
Causes of Occupational Stress

Abstract In this chapter, the causes of occupational stress, the different circumstances and diverse demands of managers' work conditions, and the relationship between the various dimensions of occupational stress are elaborated on.

Keywords Remuneration · Technology · Work and life circumstances questionnaire (WLQ) · Interviews · Surveys

It is important to understand what factors contribute to occupational stress of managers. Van Zyl and Van der Walt (1991) found with their development of the *Work and Life Circumstances Questionnaire (WLQ)* that occupational stress is dependent on three factors, namely circumstances, expectations and experiences. Oosthuizen (2016) further explored the applicability of each of these factors in the new world of work, and to find the multidimensional features of these three factors. This was done by interviewing 10 managers, and for them to complete the WLQ survey. Each of these factors are discussed in this chapter, and includes various sub-dimensions as found by the study of Oosthuizen (2016).

3.1 Circumstances and Demands

The circumstances factor pertains to the work context of the manager and accordingly indicates the level of stress experienced by an individual due to his or her work circumstances. Quick, Quick, Nelson, and Hurrell (1997) identified four broad categories of workplace demands. The first demand is task demands which include workload, careers, occupation and job insecurity. The second demand is role demands which include which includes role conflict and role ambiguity. The third demand is physical demands which include workplace design, temperature and lighting. The fourth demand is interpersonal demands which includes personality conflicts, social density, group pressures and leadership styles (Ganster & Rosen, 2013). When exploring the causes of occupational stress, three aspects of demands direct one's attention: home-based or family issues, work and occupational aspects and individually-generated or

N. MH. Carrim et al., *Occupational Stress in South African Work Culture*, SpringerBriefs in Psychology, https://doi.org/10.1007/978-981-33-6397-7_3

internally imposed elements. Within the workplace the lack of freedom of employee decisions is challenging in high strain jobs, that is, jobs that are highly demanding and low in control. The second leading reason is uncertainty about workplace elements. Job insecurity and questions related to one's actions cause chronic strain on the employee which in the long run leads to physical wear and tear. The third cause of occupational stress in the workplace is conflict that is poorly managed in the workplace (Hopkins & Yonker, 2015). The following features of work circumstances were found.

3.1.1 *Aspect of Past Life that Is Embarrassing*

Managers may feel embarrassed with previous discretions and it may influence their current work circumstances. Some of these discretions may be poor performance in a previous job or a criminal record. It was found that the longer you are with a company, the less embarrassing elements may occur for yourself but the more observant you are of others' behaviours that may be construed as embarrassing. Managers also feel they need to take ownership of their subordinates behaviours, therefore, it they misbehave, the more responsible you feel pertaining to others' behaviours.

3.1.2 *Effectively Working Overtime*

The workplace provides a combination of both demands and pressures that cause stress; hence, it is vital for the physiological and psychological health of employees to have an effective manner in which to deal with these stressors. Managers are usually expected to work overtime (Carrim, 2019) and it was found that during the week it seems to be more acceptable, while expecting to work over weekends are detrimental for their long-term health. Most managers who have families feel weekends are personal time to spend with their hobbies and their families, while during the week it is easier to put in extra time.

3.1.3 *External Stressors*

External stressors can have an either direct or indirect impact on managers in their immediate work environment. The economics instability across the world is seen as a major external stressor for employment, especially for financial sustainability. Managers need to aware of this stressor, but also, what it means to his or her employees. This conscious awareness may put more pressure on the manager. With globalisation, managers also need to understand the labour legislation of the country they are functioning in; otherwise, they can be in big trouble if they do not understand or comply with the stipulations. Managers are also responsible of their subordinates, and as a manager, you do not always have control of the conduct and behaviours of your subordinates pertaining to choices they are making (Carrim, 2019). The conduct of others also effect the manager and provide added stress to their performance. A large amount of work as well as environmental stressors can trigger the stress response. While demands can vary some occupational stress traverse occupations (Quick & Henderson, 2016). Work-life issues also add to occupational stress as demands from the home spill over into the workplace. Hammer, Kossek, Anger, Bodner, and Zimmerman (2011) focused on work-life conflict and how it increases occupational stress for employees.

3.1.4 Impact of Health on Career and Personal Aspirations

Employee health is perceived as twofold, namely physiological health and psychological health. The impact of an employee's physiological and psychological health on his/her career and personal aspirations can be a major source of stress. In this regard, ill-health can be ascribed to either external causes, such as a car accident or traumatic experience, or, on the other hand, be caused by occupational stress which is a causal agent in physical and mental disorders. If an individual experiences excessive occupational stress, one is more likely to develop bad habits such as drinking and smoking in an attempt to cope with the pressures and demands at work.

3.1.5 Impact of Life Stage on Work

The age of the manager has an impact on the cause of occupational stress and how the manager is able to cope. Not only age, but also the life stage of a manager (i.e. young married; married with children; ages of children; etc.) also has an impact. Given this fact, it is of the utmost importance for companies to understand at what life stage their employees are and how this will affect their experience of occupational stress. Managers with young children tend to be more stressed about their work demands, than managers without children or managers with older children. Managers without children have more freedom to pursue their career and keep to the demands of their work. It was also found the older the manager and the longer they are with a company and in their position, the more able they are to adapt and cope with unexpected work demands.

3.1.6 *Work-Life Balance (Leisure, Work and Personal Life)*

Given the complexity of achieving and maintaining a healthy work-life balance, it is important to assess whether work-life balance is possible for managers. In her study, Oosthuizen (2016) explored whether personal circumstances have an impact on work commitments, and vice versa. The results indicate that most managers are able to keep their personal life separate from their professional lives, except for when something unexpected happens in their personal or professional life. Then is becomes more challenging to cope, depending on the support you have at home and work.

3.1.7 *Satisfaction with Remuneration and Working Conditions*

It is common knowledge that the more competitively remuneration packages are structured and the more conducive the working conditions are, the more satisfied and evidently productive employees will be. Most managers indicate they are satisfied with their remuneration (or perceive it as fair) when extra benefits are included, for instance more leave functions (i.e. vacation, family responsibility, etc.), or flexible work hours.

3.1.8 *Technological Changes*

Continuous technological changes are the order of the day in the twenty-first century of work. Technology can be a company's biggest competitive edge or biggest downfall. Most managers are positive about the impact of technology on their work, since its advancement reduce time spend on administration. If managers are adequately trained, technology advances can actually be a contributor to less stress, while managers who adapt slowly and resist technological advancement, may have more stress.

3.2 Expectations

Expectations is the second factor of occupational stress. It indicates the level of stress experienced by an individual due to his or her expectations of the work environment (Van Zyl & Van der Walt, 1991). The following sub-dimensions of expectations were derived.

3.2.1 Ability to Take the Initiative

Individuals in managerial positions place a lot of emphasis on the extent to which their role allows them to apply their minds in performing their tasks. In the instances where managerial employees do not feel that they have enough freedom to take the initiative in solving problems and developing new concepts, emotions such as frustration and finally occupational stress will result. Most managers indicate time constraints and increasingly work demands make it impossible to be innovative in their work. For instance, a manager in charge of technical administration and legislative compliance can find it difficult to develop or implement new processes.

3.2.2 Relationship and Communication with Superior

If there is mutual respect and trust relationship between a direct superior and manager (subordinate), less occupational stress may be experienced. Furthermore, if the superior provides clear instructions, is approachable and is consistent in his or her conduct, then the manager will not experience high levels of occupational stress. However, if the relationship is negative, the superior less approachable and the message ambiguous, occupational stress will be experienced. Hence, the more concisely superiors communicate their expectations, the less stress employees experience as they comprehend what is expected of them in order to perform at an optimal level.

3.2.3 Involved in Decision-Making

Decision-making comprises a part of all managers' routine tasks, irrespective of the level of management. Involvement in decision-making is however determined by the level of management the individual fulfils. Managers bear the heavy burden of making optimal decisions, sometimes without enough time and resources to make an informed decision regarding an aspect that affects the value and viability of the organisation. It is evident that this responsibility of the organisation's longevity will have a direct impact on the individuals' level of occupational stress. The autonomy a manager has the less occupational stress they will experience. However, the less autonomy a manager has pertaining to decision-making, the more occupational stress they will experience.

3.2.4 *Mentoring and Coaching*

Executive mentoring and coaching are interventions to assist managers improve their performance and ultimately increase the overall performance of the organisation. Most managers indicate that if they have an onsite or external mentor or coach, they are more able to deal with occupational stressors. The reason may be because they have a sounding board on which they can bounce off ideas should they be unsure when faced with certain situations.

3.2.5 *Ownership of Work*

It is conventional wisdom that employees will take better care of, and work towards maintaining and nurturing, their own possessions. In this same sense, organisations need to aim to instil in their employees this motivation to continuously safeguard and improve the organisation. In order to achieve this, senior management should create a feeling that employees are responsible for making decisions that will have a long-term effect on the company. Managers, who experience ownership of their work, will be more effective and open to work longer hours. However, if it is not probably managed, and work-life interference (as oppose to work-life enrichment) is experienced, the sense of ownership will dwindle.

3.2.6 *Team Work*

In the modern age of work, work teams have become a particularly popular work design across all industries. Research indicates that managerial employees play a vital role in how team members perceive the team and their specific role in it. Oosthuizen (2016) found that managers' perceive teamwork as conducive to success, as it allows for people from different backgrounds, expertise and skills to contribute towards the same goal.

3.2.7 *Recognition for Performance*

Regardless of the position or job level, appropriate recognition for a job well done is a strong motivator. Human beings inherently have a predisposition to increase their effort if the reward is worth their while, whether it be verbal or monetary recognition. Verbal recognition goes a long way for managers (Oosthuizen, 2016), while a monetary incentive is always welcome. It was also found the higher the internal locus of control, the more internalised the reward is (i.e. having pride; satisfaction, etc.), while external locus of control individuals prefer observable recognition practices.

3.3 Experiences

Experiences is the last factor. It indicates the level of stress of the individual, and whether the individual experiences stress at normal, high or very high levels (Van Zyl & Van der Walt, 1991). The following features were identified.

3.3.1 Boredom and Challenging Work Circumstances

Automation has become all the more prevalent across various work domains, where human manual work has decreased and human supervision of automated processes has increased. The automation of increasingly more complex systems means that boredom is no longer caused only by monotonous and repetitive tasks, but also by low task loading. However, when considering a complex task such as decision-making and problem solving, which are key tasks in most managerial positions, automation has not yet reached that level of cognizance. Routine and administrative tasks for managers are frustrating since it is not seen as stimulating work. Automation may in future take away most of these tasks from the manager, but the repetitive tasks can be seen as strenuous and daunting.

3.3.2 Career Progression and the Glass Ceiling

Career progression is a life-long journey of managing learning and work. Career progression is a continuous process and takes place throughout an individual's various life stages. Not all employees see promotion as progression in their career, but are rather focused on building their skills and have enriched projects and experiences. When considering the career progression of female employees, the "glass ceiling" is considered one of the most prevalent descriptions for analysing inequalities between men and women in the workplace. In the modern age of work, women even more find it easier to get through the front door of managerial hierarchies, however, there does come a point where their upward movement is blocked by an invisible barrier.

3.3.3 Conflict Handling

Conflict is inevitable in any work environment. Employees come from different backgrounds and cultures; it is not a question of whether, but when, conflict will arise. Hence, it is of the utmost importance for managers to be able to deal with conflict in a constructive manner.

3.3.4 *Delegating Work to Subordinates*

Delegation of work is the transfer of authority to make decisions and complete particular tasks. In a pressurised work environment, the ability to delegate is one of the most vital skills for managers to possess. Strong delegation skills can save managers a lot of time; they can train and motivate their subordinates, avoid burnout and enable managers to take on new opportunities. However, on the negative side of delegating, managers may find it frustrating when subordinates do not follow instructions, or do not conduct the work efficiently. Therefore, it may increase the occupational stress of managers.

3.3.5 *Short-Tempered*

The workplace is one of the greatest stressors experienced by human beings. Stress can manifest in many ways that may be positive, negative or neutral and that may have an effect on an individual's physical and psychological well-being. One of the negative and all-so-common realisations of excessive occupational stress is irritability or a short-temper.

3.3.6 *Work Overload*

Work overload is seen as the bulk of the hours, the sacrifice of time and the sense of frustration an individual experiences accompanied by the inability of the individual to complete tasks within a specific period. Work overload is generally known to be one of the leading stressors in the modern age of work. It was found in the current study that managerial employees value job autonomy and that a lack thereof causes occupational stress.

3.4 Other Causes of Occupational Stress

Beside the above-mentioned causes of occupational stress, past research has also identified numerous reasons why employees experience high levels of stress in organisations.

Job satisfaction as an indicator of occupational stress has revealed that role ambiguity (Faucett, Corwyn, & Poling, 2012), role overload (Correa & Ferreira, 2011) and work-family conflict (Chen, Huang, & Su, 2012) have been shown as predictors of job dissatisfaction. Role overload has been shown to be a source of occupational stress and acts as a major negative predictor of job satisfaction and a positive predictor of negative emotions at work. Employees at various levels have been studied to predict the relationship between job satisfaction and role overload (Correa & Ferreira, 2011; Rai, 2013; Zainudin, Junaidah, & Nazmi, 2010).

Correa and Ferriera (2011) indicate that employees who feel that they were expected to work in positions with greater demands than their own abilities tended to be less satisfied in their jobs and feel more negative toward their jobs. A study by Kemery (2006) indicated that although role ambiguity and role conflict were negatively related to job satisfaction, their combined effect on appointment satisfaction was even more complex. When role ambiguity and role conflict are both high, appointment satisfaction was low but when role conflict was low, satisfaction was high when role ambiguity was high.

Women in the workplace experience high levels of stress due to their dual roles at home and the workplace which leads to occupational stress. On the one hand women as employees are required to display their best performance for the organisation and they are expected to be super women at home as well (Irawanto, Noermiyati, & Primasari, 2015).

Elements such as workload (either underload or overload, low work autonomy, high work pace (time pressures), absence of job meaningfulness, toxic work systems, external disturbances (such as overcrowding and noise)) and are some examples that can pose health damage and disrupt well-being of employees engaged in such poor working conditions. Other sources of occupational stress Occupational stress occurs in managerial roles which include with higher levels of responsibilities without clear delineations of role boundaries or where employees have to answer to diverse demands from supervisors and others within the organisation in a simultaneous but unrealistic manner. When this is the case, such employees undergo role stress which are composed of role conflict and role ambiguity. Role ambiguity is a situation where employees see a lack of important information and role clarity that is needed to perform the work role effectively, while role conflict occurs when the job's expectations and demands from the employee's supervisors, peers, are incongruent and incompatible (Ackfeldt & Malhotra, 2013).

Another category of contextual stressors stems from elements that weaken career development. In this category stress-related issues that commence from lack of job security sometimes have the potential of negatively impacting career progress and may have a detrimental effect on employees' commitment and sense of wellbeing (Akanji, 2013). For instance, the perpetual changes in the nature of work as a result of technological advancements used in modern workplaces in order to improve the performance of workplaces and sustain competitive advantage has resulted to the growth of non-permanent contracts and contingent work arrangements which are caused by outsourcing, downsizing, acquisitions and mergers, delayering, re-organising work schedules, to handle the pace of global technological advancement and global competition (Kossek, Kalliath, & Kalliath, 2012). Hence, these changes in modern working life have produced stressful workplaces that have led to job insecurity, low job autonomy, low promotion rates and has even created situations where the employee in unable to advance in his/her career (Colligan & Higgins, 2005).

Another category that contributes to workplace stress is the existing work relationships within the workplace. Challenging relationships among subordinates, managers and peers in the form of threats of violence, office bullying, harassment, artificial physical and social workplace isolation, dark leadership and other deviant behaviours often cause social disruptions and could possibly generate outcomes that range from passive to active dislike, disrespect, animosity or destructive mutual interactions within the workplace (Akanji, 2013). The final category relates to formalisation which relates to employees' roles within the organisation which are standardised and are guided by rules and regulations. Where jobs are highly formalised employees have little autonomy and to do their work and have to face rigid rules and procedures and this leads to inappropriate locus of control needs for work demands (Akanji, 2013).

3.5 Relationship Between the Dimensions of Occupational Stress

In this section, the relationship between the three dimensions of occupational stress is explored. According to Oosthuizen (2016), it seems when the stressors increase in the domains of work expectation, the stressors will also increase in the work circumstances domains. This can be attributed to the fact that employees' expectations and realities in their employment roles differ, therefore the stress experienced due to the expectations of individuals' work environment and their actual work circumstances vary (Oosthuizen, 2016).

Furthermore, Oosthuizen (2016) found that the work experiences and work circumstances have a definite positive effect on one another. Thus, it has been found that the manner in which individuals experience their work circumstances has a definite impact on their occupational stress levels. Hence, the inference is made that as the stressors increase in an individual's work circumstances, accordingly that person's level of stress experienced will also increase.

Lastly, Oosthuizen (2016) mentioned that a general finding is made that a significant positive relationship exists between work circumstances and work expectations. Thus, the greater the discrepancy between individuals' expectations of their work and the actual work circumstances they find themselves in, the more stress the individual will perceive. This is a significant finding as the Oosthuizen (2016) could not find any literature substantiating that a discrepancy between an individual's expectations and actual work circumstances would significantly increase that individual's level of occupational stress. Hence, the observation is made that individuals with an internal WLOC will experience higher levels of occupational stress when there is a definite discrepancy between their expectations and the realities of their working life. Oosthuizen (2016) is of the opinion that this finding can be attributed to the fact that internals are characterised for taking control over their circumstances and that their inability to marry their expectations and actual circumstances can cause frustration and evidently increase their level of occupational stress. This outcome can potentially also have an impact on the internal individual's attitudes and behaviours, such as performance (Erez & Judge, 2001) and job satisfaction (Muhonen & Torkelson, 2004).

3.6 Summary of Chapter 3

This Chapter provided a deeper understanding of Occupational Stress. All three factors of the WLQ were found to consist of many different sub-dimensions. Therefore, although the factors (Consequences, Expectation, and Experiences) encompasses the essence of Occupational Stress, its content is quite broad and comprehensive. Now that the causes of Occupational Stress is known, it is important to be more aware of the consequences of Occupational Stress for the individual and organisation. This will be discussed in the next Chapter.

References

Ackfeldt, A., & Malhotra, N. (2013). Revisiting the role stress-commitment relationship: Can managerial interventions help? *European Journal of Marketing, 47*(3), 1–37.

Akanji, B. (2013). Occupational stress: A review on conceptualisations causes and cure. *Economic Insights, 2*(3), 73–80.

Carrim, N. M. H. (2019). The in-betweeners: Racioethnic and masculine identity work of Indian male managers in the South African private sector. *The Journal of Men's Studies, 27*(1), 3–23.

Chen, T. L., Huang, M. Y., & Su, T. H. (2012). Work motivation, work stress, and job satisfaction in between Taiwan and China–An empirical study. *World Academy of Science, Engineering and Technology, 68*, 1446–1450.

Colligan, T. W., & Higgins, E. M. (2005). Workplace stress: Etiology and consequences. *Journal of Workplace Health, 21*(2), 90–97.

Correa, A. P., & Ferreira, M. C. (2011). The impact of environmental stressors and types of work contract on occupational stress. *The Spanish Journal of Psychology, 14*(1), 251–262.

Erez, A., & Judge, T. A. (2001). Relationship of core self-evaluations to goal setting, motivation, and performance. *Journal of Applied Psychology, 86*, 1270–1279.

Faucett, J. M., Corwyn, R. F., & Poling, T. H. (2012). Clergy role stress: Interactive effects of role ambiguity and role conflict on intrinsic job satisfaction. *Pastoral Psychology, 62*(3), 291–304.

Ganster, D. C., & Rosen, C. C. (2013). Work stress and employee health: A multidisciplinary review. *Journal of Management, 39*(5), 1085–1122.

Hammer, L. B., Kossek, E. E., Anger, W. K., Bodner, T., & Zimmerman, K. L. (2011). Clarifying work–family intervention processes: The roles of work–family conflict and family-supportive supervisor behaviors. *Journal of Applied Psychology, 96*(1), 134–145.

Hopkins, M. M., & Yonker, R. D. (2015). Managing conflict with emotional intelligence: Abilities that make a difference. *Journal of Management Development, 32*(2), 226–244.

Irawanto, D. W., Noermiyati, & Primasari, D. (2015). The effect of occupational stress on work performance of female employees: Study in Indonesia. *Asia-Pacific Journal of Management Research and Innovation, 11*(4), 336–345.

Kemery, E. R. (2006). Clergy role stress and satisfaction: Role ambiguity isn't always bad. *Pastoral Psychology, 54*(6), 561–570.

Kossek, E. E., Kalliath, T., & Kalliath, P. (2012). Achieving employee wellbeing in a changing work environment: An expert commentary on current scholarship. *International Journal of Manpower, 33*(7), 738–753.

Muhonen, T., & Torkelson, E. (2004). Work locus of control and its relationship to health and job satisfaction from a gender perspective. *Stress and Health, 20,* 21–28.

Oosthuizen, M. M. (2016). *The relationship between occupational stress and Work Locus of Control amongst South African management: An exploratory study.* Unpublished MCom dissertation, University of Pretoria, Pretoria, South Africa.

Quick, J. C., & Henderson, D. F. (2016). Occupational stress: Preventing suffering, enhancing wellbeing. *International Journal of Environmental Research and Public Health, 13*(5), 459–465.

Quick, J. C., Quick, J. D., Nelson, D. L., & Hurrell, J. J. (1997). *Preventive stress management in organizations.* Washington, DC: American Psychological Association.

Rai, G. S. (2013). Job satisfaction among long-term care staff: Bureaucracy isn't always bad. *Administration in Social Work, 37*(1), 90–99.

Van Zyl, E. S., & Van der Walt, H. S. (1991). *Manual for the experience of work and life circumstances questionnaire (WLQ).* Pretoria, South Africa: Human Sciences Research Council.

Zainudin, A., Junaidah, H. A., & Nazmi, M. Z. (2010). Modeling job satisfaction and work commitment among lecturers: A case of UITM Kelantan. *Journal of Statistical Modeling and Analytics, 1*(2), 45–59.

Chapter 4
Consequences of Occupational Stress

Abstract This chapter outlines the consequences of occupational stress. The negative and positive outcomes of occupational stress are explored on an individual and organisational level. Evidence of how employees and organisations cope with stress will conclude this Chapter.

Keywords Negative stress effects · Positive stress effects · Coping with stress · Organisational effects of stress

Stress effects individuals differently, and may have positive or negative consequences, given the person's resilience and management of stress. During the global crisis the work environment is challenged and re-structured pertaining to COVID-19, therefore, stress may have dire consequences if not handled constructively for the person and for the organisation.

4.1 Negative Effects of Stress

Past research has indicated that occupational stress leads to numerous negative consequences for employees and the workplace (Narahari & Koneru, 2017). Factors that lead to negative work experiences such as occupational stress generate negative work outcomes (Lopopolo, 2002). Stress creates a variety of expensive, unwanted and devastating consequences which affects both employees and the workplace. The negative consequences of occupational stress comprise a decrease in productivity, decreased levels of customer service, turnover, absenteeism, alcohol and drug abuse, accidents and deliberate destructive behaviours. Occupational stress also leads to migraines, heart attacks, headaches, blood pressure and so on (Yahaya, Yahaya, Tamyes, Ismail, & Jaalam, 2010).

Research indicates that employees suffering from stress are more likely to have more job dissatisfaction, they engage in negative psychological symptoms, increase in drinking and smoking, increased absenteeism and decreased self-esteem and inspirations (Jayashree, 2010).

N. MH. Carrim et al., *Occupational Stress in South African Work Culture*, SpringerBriefs in Psychology, https://doi.org/10.1007/978-981-33-6397-7_4

Past research has also indicated that employees experiencing stress display an increase in accidents, more interpersonal conflicts with supervisors and peers and lower morale, take more time off (Narahari & Koneru, 2017).

Studies also indicate that occupational negatively impacts that immune system and increases the likelihood of the common flu. Many organisations have introduced wellness and health promotion programs as part of stress management interventions. However, the effectiveness of these programs have been questioned as they target employees and their ways of coping with stressful situations rather than ascertaining the causes of stress that are integral in the workplace and the kind of work that employees do. Intense and prolonged stress has a negative effect on the physical and mental health of individuals (Narahari & Koneru, 2017). Hakim and Sutrisno (2018) conducted a study of 135 contract employees in an organisation in Java investigating how occupational stress impacts organisational commitment, job satisfaction and turnover intention. The results of their study indicated that occupational stress results in employee turnover, job dissatisfaction and decreased organisational commitment.

4.2 Individual and Organisational Level Stress

The consequences of occupational stress can be clustered into individual and organisational levels.

4.2.1 Individual Level

At the individual level there are three main subgroups of strains: The first consequence of occupational stress at the individual level is *unwanted feelings and behaviours* that include lower motivation, job dissatisfaction, decreased organisational commitment, decreased employee morale, absenteeism, decreased quality of life, intention to leave the job, absenteeism, decreased productivity, decreased quality and quantity of work, increased levels of theft, inability to make sound decisions, work stoppage, sabotage, alienation, burnout, increase in alcohol intake and smoking (Narahari & Koneru, 2017; Pramode, 2019). Studies on occupational stress and job burnout indicate that occupational stress predicts job burnout (Meyer, Li, Klaristenfeld, & Gold, 2015), while coping style plays a regulatory role in the relationship between the two An increase in workload also increases occupational stress, which leads to job burnout (Lasalvia & Tansella, 2011). There are many examples within various countries related to ccupational stress related to causing employee turnover. A few examples from different countries follow that illustrate how occupational stress leads to employee turnover. A study by Zahra, Khan, Imran, Aman, and Ali (2018) indicate that occupational stress is present in all unpleasant situations in the workplace. The authors selected twelve organisations with a total of 412 employees in Pakistan and found that a lack of support from supervisors, work overload and work ambiguity resulted in high levels of occupational stress and which led to high employee turnover. A study conducted by Mosadeghrad (2013) in Iran among 296 nurses found that occupational stress was increased due to heavy workloads, discrimination at work, lack of promotion, insufficient pay, job insecurity, staff scarcity and a lack of support from management which increased the intention to leave the hospital among staff. Similarly, Arshadi and Damiri (2013) conducted a study on 286 employees from a drilling company in Iran. The authors found that the intention to leave the organisation was high among staff due to occupational stress related to issues of a lack of self-esteem and high levels of productivity expectations. Pramode (2019) found in their study of 55 employees in a Chennai organisation that 91% of occupational stress factors led to employee turnover.

The second consequence of occupational stress at the individual level is *physiological disease or poor health* and manifests as the physical reaction of the body to the stressful situation. Symptoms associated with the physical reaction of the body to occupational stress include lethargy, migraines, abdominal pains, backaches, fatigue, chest pains, heart palpitations, muscle aches, disturbances and changes in drinking, eating, smoking and sleeping habits caused by various triggers in the workplace (Manshor, Fontaine, & Ching, 2003). Other physical symptoms of occupational stress include but are not limited to an increased pulse rate, increased blood pressure, high cholesterol, cardiovascular diseases, headaches, insomnia, high blood sugar, skin problems, suppressed immune system, fatigue and injuries (Ashong, Rogers, Botwe, & Anim-Sampong, 2016; Narahari & Koneru, 2016). Psychosocial issues can lead to injury, illness, isolation, stigmatisation and even death. They also lead to decrease in morale and negatively impact productivity.

The third consequence of occupational stress at the individual level, is *psychological diseases* caused by psychological stress and is seen as an emotional reaction such as poor mental and emotional health. Symptoms of these include anxiousness, psychological distress, boredom, aggressiveness, depression, nervousness, passiveness, loss of self-esteem and confidence, feelings of futility, burnout, frustration, anger, tension, irritability, job alienation, loss of concentration, hostility, a disregard for social values and norms, impulsiveness, emotional fatigue, a loss of contact with reality and dissatisfaction with life and one's job (Millward, 2005; Narahari & Koneru, 2017). Occupational stress has also resulted in employees undergoing psychiatric care (Adenuga, 2015). For example, in the United Kingdom there is a high incidence of men suffering from personality disorders and psychoneurotic symptoms, migraine headaches, nervousness and smoking as well as 22.8 million work days being absent from work (Felton & Cole, 2010). Smith (2011) asserted that due to occupational stress disease among industrial workers is increasing and these diseases manifest during work life as well as in retirement.

Employees who cannot control occupational stress in their work environments will display negative work attitudes (Seaward, 2005). Employees who are unable to control occupational stress are unable to manage and control their psychological and physiological stresses and the result is that such employees may not perform their responsibilities and duties as members of their organisations (Critchley et al., 2005). Past research indicates that occupational stress has a major impact on employees' job performance and health and can lead to anxiety (Cole, 2010; Rechel, Buchan, & McKee, 2009). This assertion has led researchers like Davies (2012) to view occupational stress stemming from an employee's relationship with the supervisor that negatively impacts a worker's productivity and efficiency.

Most past research on occupational stress has been conducted in the healthcare industry (Van Niekerk, 2011) as the workload of healthcare professionals are high. However, recently research on occupational stress has been conducted in diverse industries to ascertain the individual and organisational factors leading to occupational stress. For example, Adenuga (2015) conducted a study on occupational stress in the banking industry. In recent times due to globalisation bank employees are experiencing tremendous amounts of occupational stress, where each employee's workload has increased and they are expected to do four staff members' jobs. The result is that tasks are not completed efficiently and effectively as workers having an extremely high workload which negatively impacts their mental health (Alawiye, 2014).

Researchers indicate that there exists a link between mental health and workers' occupational stress in the workplace environment (Azeez & Adenuga, 2009). Pearlstein et al. (2006) point out that mental health is a psychological state of wellbeing, a sense of purpose in life, growth, positive relations with others and self-acceptance. Iorvaa (2004) sees mental health as an individual's adjustment to himself/herself and to society so that the individual can face the reality of life and function effectively in a happy, satisfying and acceptable manner. Thus, individuals with a mental illness do not believe in themselves, they are not able to cope with problems that they encounter daily in their lives, they distrust other people, and they have problems relating to others (Adenuga, 2015). According to Moronkola (2003) the following are elements that characterise good mental health: a person having the ability to forgive others and the self, the individual considering other people's interest as well as their own self-interest, the individual respecting others' rights and opinions and handling problems as they occur. The individual having the ability to believe in themselves and pursuing worthwhile ideals, setting realistic goals, thinking through and making rational decisions and being part of a worthwhile group as well as spending quality leisure time and sleeping without worries. Adenuga's (2015) study in Nigeria banks on 100 employees also revealed that there is a relationship between occupational stress and mental health and job satisfaction. Employees with high occupational stress experienced job dissatisfaction and high levels of mental health issues.

An interesting finding by Taylor et al. (2000) relates to occupational stress experienced by male and female employees. The authors discovered that women has an attitude of "tend and befriend". This attitude accounts for female employees outperforming male employees in dealing with occupational stress and hence outliving males by five to seven years. Women also tend to perform repetitive tasks and are more exposed to stress due to unpaid work, which can result in more work-related upper extremity disorders (Lundberg, 2002).

There are certain individual difference factors that lead to either increasing vulnerability to occupational stress or protecting against the risks associated with it. The first factor is vulnerability. Three individual differences increase vulnerability, namely, Type A or coronary-prone behaviour, competitiveness, time urgency, quantification of achievements and hostility; lower socioeconomic status which results in an individual coming into contact with many diseases and social isolation (Quick & Henderson, 2016).

Protection is another individual factor which includes self-reliance. Self-reliance focuses on strong interdependent relationships with others which can result in a care giving system or attachment. Secure relationships are a basis of information, instrumental support, evaluative feedback and emotional strength. Personality hardiness which is characterised by control, commitment and challenge also provide protection as a stress-resistance element (Quick, Joplin, Nelson, Mangelsdorff, & Fiedler, 1996). Injuries also causes death, while injuries at work and the associated pain leads to high levels of absenteeism.

Psychological distress which includes depression and anxiety are as a result of occupational stress in the workplace. Mood and anxiety disorders are common for employees who experience high levels of occupational stress. Depression is one of the biggest contributors to lost productivity and morbidity (Gatchel & Kishino, 2011). Burnout is another form of psychological distress. Maslach (2006) regarded burnout as emotional exhaustion, cynicism or depersonalisation and lack of personal accomplishment. Privitera, Rosenstein, Plessow, and LoCastro (2015) indicate that burnout can be defined on several levels. Firstly, *exhaustion-* that is, emotional and physical downward spiral even after one tries and rests. Secondly, *depersonalisation-* dysfunctional copying mechanism in keeping one's distance from colleagues so that one does not feel more drained. Behaviour that manifest sarcasm, cynicism and compassion fatigue (nothing left to give). Thirdly, *lack of efficacy-* work has no purpose and a feeling that work is subpar.

There are different forms of behavioural distress which includes alcohol, tobacco and drug abuse, violence, aggression and accidents. Alcohol abuse negatively impacts task performance, attendance, injuries and accidents (Kaplan & Tetrick, 2011). Drug abuse includes disability, lost productivity, withdrawal from the workforce and death.

4.2.2 Organisational Level

Workplace violence and aggression has also increased in the workplace due to distress and industrial accidents cause distress and are the main cause of death for men in organisations (Nelson & Simmons, 2011).

The consequences of stress on the *organisational level* can be grouped into two groups. The first consequence of occupational stress at the organisational level is *organisational symptoms* which include unhappiness and low morale among employees, poor quality services and products, a loss in performance and productivity, poor relationships with partners, suppliers, customers and regulatory authorities, damaging the corporate reputation and image, bad publicity, disrupting production, missed opportunities, high labour turnover, losing customers, increased mistakes and accident rates, losing valuable employees, constant vacancies, increased sick leave, decreased cooperation, premature retirement, poor internal communication, decreased cooperation, dysfunctional organisational climate and increase in internal conflicts (Ashong et al., 2016; Narahari & Koneru, 2017). Ashong et al. (2016) report that occupational stress is high in Ghana as the healthcare system has a lack of adequate personnel, the equipment is outdated and functions poorly, the working hours are long, employees are exposed to infectious diseases and hazardous substances, there are threats of malpractice and litigation and employees are constantly reminded of death and dying. The authors reported that although the working hours of radiographers is 40 hours per week, the majority work many more hours a day due to the work load. The result is that radiographers in the country have decreased by 30% due to the occupational stress associated with long work hours. The results of the 122 radiographers who took part in Ashong et al.'s (2016) study revealed that job dissatisfaction, sick leave and depression were caused by occupational stress due to extremely high workloads.

The second consequence of occupational stress at the organisational level is *organizational costs* which include increased sick pay, decreased productivity and performance in terms of a decrease in added value to services and products, increase in disability payments and health-care costs, increase in grievances, compensation and litigation costs, high labour turnover replacement costs due to an increase in training, recruitment and retaining costs and increased equipment damage costs (Narahari & Koneru, 2017). With regards to employee turnover due to occupational stress, Pramode (2019) point out two costs incurred by the organisation. The first cost which are direct costs, relate to recruitment, selection and placement of employees and loss of work time. The second cost, which are indirect costs that these authors identify relate to a decrease in organisational performance.

4.3 Coping with Stress

Beside the psychological and physical consequences of occupational stress, the effects of behavioural, psychological and social strains at the occupational stress levels have resulted in job dissatisfaction, depersonalisation, boredom, anxiety, depression, somatic complaints and emotional exhaustion (Narahari & Koneru, 2017). The outcomes of occupational stress can lead to major social and economic costs for both employers and employees and can result in increased internal conflicts, absenteeism rates and low employee morale (Botha & Pienaar, 2006).

Employees in different industries use different methods of coping with stress. In Ashong et al.'s (2016) study radiographers indicated that they use conventional coping mechanism to deal with the high workload in hospitals.

Stress interventions benefit individual employees, the workplace and then both the employee and the organisation. These types of interventions have been theorised as primary, secondary and tertiary management interventions (SMIs). Primary interventions focus on decreasing, modifying or eliminating tensioned work demands that have a negative impact on performance and health (Lamontagne, Keegel, Louie, Ostry, & Landsbergis, 2007). An example s job redesign that reduces stress, organisational culture that focuses on employee wellness and labour flexibility practices. Secondary interventions assist employees to cope with work stress and include planned social events, wellness programs, stress management training and development, provision of recreational facilities (Lamontagne et al., 2007). Tertiary interventions are therapeutic in nature and are focused on assisting employees who exhibit symptoms and signs of sickness and other adversarial outcomes due to occupational stress (Lamontagne et al., 2007).

Remedial actions such as employee assistance programs, counselling, payments on injury claims and rehabilitation sessions can assist employees suffering from occupational stress. Proactive interventions that remove or eliminate occupational stress are more rewarding than decreasing or treating manifested health issues. The cost of absenteeism, poor performance, turnovers and sickness are much higher when one compares the investment cost in keeping employees healthy, well and present by implementing primary rather than secondary and tertiary SMIs Organisations should therefore focus on primary interventions to prevent occupational stress from occurring (Lamontagne et al., 2007).

It is therefore imperative that proactive interventions become part of the structural context of the organisation (for example, work schedules, physical work environments, job control and organisational structure) and the psychological frame of workers (for example, psychological support, job commitment, employee engagement and affective wellbeing initiatives). Also, primary measures such as managerial stress awareness training, hazard identification, workload adjustments, creation of social structures that decrease stress effects and role clarification are strategies that can be implemented and are effective and will result in better organisational outcomes. From a practical perspective working conditions should be adapted to the differences in employees in terms of their physical, mental and contextual life circumstances. Organisations should also pay more attention to the work-life balance (WLB) of their employees by trying to implement diverse WLB policies and practices such as job sharing, flexitime, home telecommuting, part-time work, subsidised recreational and leisure activities and other family-friendly policies. Adopting a more strategic approach to WLB can assist in promoting improved employee performance and better physical and mental health, reduced turnover and job satisfaction (Lamontagne et al., 2007).

Countervailing interventions are also another form of dealing with occupational stress. Countervailing interventions focus on increasing the positive aspects of work and decreasing the negative elements of the workplace. For example, it was suggested that positive development of the state of psychological capital of employees related to their self-efficacy, trust, hope, resilience and optimism is imperative for positive organisational behaviour and health which is a necessity for today's competitive world (Lamontagne et al., 2007).

4.4 Summary of Chapter 4

The negative consequences of occupational stress were highlighted. As mentioned, outcomes of occupational stress have negative outcomes for employees and for the organisation. Although this Chapter focused heavily on the individual consequences, the effects of that usually has bigger implications for organisation if not managed properly. Coping with occupational stress is different for each employee, and is dependent on the extent of occupational stress. In the next Chapter, work locus of control as a possible outcome of occupational stress will be discussed.

References

Adenuga, O. A. (2015). Impact of occupational stress on job satisfaction and mental health of first bank employees: Implication for personnel psychologists. *Science, 1*(1), 15–21.

Alawiye, A. (Nigerian eye, 5th February, 2014). Bank workers live in fear as job losses continue. Available at: http://www.nigerianeye.com/2014/02/bank-workers-live-inear-as-job-losses.losses.html.

Arshadi, N., & Damiri, H. (2013). The relationship of job stress with turnover intention and job performance: Moderating role of OBSE. *Procedia-Social and Behavioral Sciences, 84,* 706–710.

Ashong, G. G. N. A., Rogers, H., Botwe, B. O., & Anim-Sampong, S. (2016). Effects of occupational stress and coping mechanisms adopted by radiographers in Ghana. *Radiography, 22*(2), 112–117.

Azeez, R. O., & Adenuga, O. A. (2009). Effects of perceived stress, self-efficacy and mental health on psychological well-being of secondary school teachers. *The Educational Psychologists, 7,* 144–152.

Botha, C., & Pienaar, J. (2006). South African correctional official occupational stress: The role of psychological strengths. *Journal of Criminal Justice, 34*(1), 73–84.

Cole, A. H. (2010). Analysis of occupational stress and employees' health conditions in manufacturing companies. *Journal of Medical Sciences, 8*(2), 78–88.

Critchley, H. D., Rotshtein, P., Nagai, Y., O'Doherty, J., Mathias, C. J., & Dolan, R. J. (2005). Activity in the human brain predicting differential heart rate responses to emotional facial expressions. *Neuroimage, 24*(3), 751–762.

Davies, V. P. (2012). Fundamentals of occupational health hazard in organizations: An empirical studies. *International Journal of Educational Psychology and developmental Studies, 5*(2), 23–34.

Gatchel, R. J., & Kishino, N. (2011). Pain, musculoskeletal injuries and return to work. In J. C. Quick & L. E. Tetrick (Eds.), *Handbook of occupational health psychology* (pp. 265–276). Washington, DC, USA: American Psychological Association.

Hakim, A. L., & Sutrisno, S. (2018). The effect of work stress on turnover intention with work satisfaction and commitment as intervening variable (Study at PT. Infomedia Solusi Humanika, Malang). *European Journal of Business and Management, 10*(12), 85–95.

Iorvaa, T. (2004). *Introduction to health education.* Makurdi, Nigeria: Adeka Publishers Company Nigeria Ltd.

Jayashree, R. (2010). Stress management with special reference to public sector bank employees in Chennai. *International Journal of Enterprise and Innovation Management Studies, 1*(3), 34–35.

Kaplan, S., & Tetrick, L. E. (2011). Workplace safety and accidents: An industrial and organizational psychology perspective. In S. Zedeck (Ed.), *Handbook of industrial and organizational psychology* (pp. 455–472). Washington, DC, USA: American Psychological Association.

Lamontagne, A. D., Keegel, T., Louie, A. M., Ostry, A., & Landsbergis, P. A. (2007). A systematic review of the job-stress intervention evaluation literature 1990–2005. *International Journal of Occupational and Environmental Health,* 13, 268–280.

Lasalvia, A., & Tansella, M. (2011). Occupational stress and job burnout in mental health. *Epidemiology and Psychiatric Sciences, 20*(04), 279–285.

Lopopolo, R. B. (2002). The relationship of role-related variables to job satisfaction and commitment to the organization in a restructured hospital environment. *Physical Therapy, 82*(10), 984–999.

Lundberg, U. (2002). Psychophysiology of work: Stress, gender, endocrine response, and work-related upper extremity disorders. *American Journal of Industrial Medicine, 41*(5), 383–392.

Manshor, A. T., Fontaine, R., & Choy, C. S. (2003). Occupational stress among managers: A Malaysian survey. *Journal of Managerial Psychology, 18*(6), 622–628.

Maslach, C. (2006). Understanding job burnout. In A. M. Rossi, P. L. Perrewe, & S. L. Sauter (Eds.), *Stress and quality of working life: Current perspectives in occupational health* (pp. 37–51). Greenwich, CT, USA: Information Age Publishing.

Meyer, R. M., Li, A., Klaristenfeld, J., & Gold, J. I. (2015). Pediatric novice nurses: Examining compassion fatigue as a mediator between stress exposure and compassion satisfaction, burnout, and job satisfaction. *Journal of Pediatric Nursing, 30*(1), 174–183.

Millward, L. J. (2005). *Understanding occupational & organizational psychology*. London, UK: Sage.

Moronkola, O. A. (2003). *Essays on issues of mental health*. Ibadan: Royal People (NIG) Ltd.

Mosadeghrad, A. M. (2013). Occupational stress and turnover intention: Implications for nursing management. *International Journal of Health Policy and Management, 1*(2), 169–179.

Narahari, C. L., & Koneru, K. (2016). Stress Management Techniques in Banking Sectors in India. *International Journal of Research in Business Studies, 2*(2): 88–100.

Narahari, C. L., & Koneru, D. K. (2017). A study on the role of occupational stress in organisations. *International Journal of Engineering Techology, Engineering, Management & Applied Science, 5,* 53–59.

Nelson, D. L., & Simmons, B. L. (2011). Savoring eustress while coping with distress: The holistic model of stress. In J. C. Quick, & L. E. Tetrick (Eds.), *Handbook of occupational health psychology* (pp. 55–74). 2nd ed. Washington, DC, USA; American Psychological Association.

Pearlstein, T. B., Zlotnick, C., Battle, C. L., Stuart, S., O'Hara, M. W., Price, A. B., et al. (2006). Patient choice of treatment for postpartum depression: A pilot study. *Archives of Women's Mental Health, 9*(6), 303–308.

Privitera, M. R., Rosenstein, A. H., Plessow, F., & LoCastro, T. M. (2015). Physician burnout and occupational stress: An inconvenient truth with unintended consequences. *Journal of Hospital Administration, 4*(1), 27–35.

Pramode, D. (2019). Effect of occupational stress on turnover intention: A study with special attention to information technology employees in Chennai. *Journal of the Gujarat Research Society, 21*(15s2), 111–118.

Quick, J. C., & Henderson, D. F. (2016). Occupational stress: Preventing suffering, enhancing wellbeing. *International Journal of Environmental Research and Public Health, 13*(5), 459–465.

Quick, J. C., Joplin, J. R., Nelson, D. L., Mangelsdorff, A. D., & Fiedler, E. (1996). Self-reliance and military service training outcomes. *Military Psychology, 8*(4), 279–293.

Rechel, B., Buchan, J., & McKee, M. (2009). The impact of health facilities on healthcare workers' well-being and performance. *International Journal of Nursing Studies, 46*(7), 1025–1034.

Seaward, B. L. (2005). *Quiet mind, fearless heart: The Taoist path through stress and spirituality*. Hoboken, NJ: John Wiley & Sons.

Smith, L. O. (2011). Workplace stress and organizational intervention programmes: An holistic approach. *Journal of Information Technology and Management, 2*(2), 45–56.

Taylor, S. E., Klein, L. C., Lewis, B. P., Gruenewald, T. L., Gurung, R. A., & Updegraff, J. A. (2000). Biobehavioral responses to stress in females: Tend-and-befriend, not fight-or-flight. *Psychological Review, 107*(3), 411–420.

Van Niekerk, M. (2011). The relationship between occupational stress and locus of control among nurses (Unpublished master's dissertation). University of Pretoria, Pretoria, South Africa.

Yahaya, N., Yahaya, A., Tamyes, F. A., Ismail, J., & Jaalam, S. (2010). The effect of various modes of occupational stress, job satisfaction, intention to leave and absenteeism companies commission of Malaysia. *Australian Journal of Basic and Applied Sciences, 4*(7), 1676–1684.

Zahra, S. S., Khan, M. I., Imran, M., Aman, Q., & Ali, R. (2018). The relationship between job stress and turnover intentions in the pesticide sector of Pakistan: An employee behavior perspective. *Management Issues in Healthcare System, 4,* 1–12.

Chapter 5
Work Locus of Control of Managers

Abstract In this chapter, the foundation and theories of work locus of control are explored and their applicability to managers. Various definitions of work of control are evident which provides an in-depth understanding of the concept. The different levels and domains of work locus of control are discussed in order to provide managers the necessary sources to manage occupational stress.

Keywords Internal work locus of control · External work locus of control · Dimensionality of work locus of control · Domain-specific work locus of control · Social learning theory · Attribution theory

5.1 Origin and Conceptualisation of Work Locus of Control

The construct "locus of control" originated from the social learning theory (Rotter, 1966). Rotter (1966) mentioned that locus of control is oriented from internal and external stimuli. He stated that when a person follows actions motivated by self and the social environment of functioning, and see outcomes as purely based on luck, chance, fate, as under the control of a powerful other, or as unpredictable because of the great complexity of the forces surrounding the person, then the person has a strong external locus of control. If the person perceives that the event is contingent upon their own behaviour or their own relatively permanent characteristics, Rotter has termed this belief as an internal locus of control.

Rotter (1966) originally defined LOC as a generalised belief concerning the exigency between one's actions and actual outcome. Social learning mechanisms (Lu, Wu, & Cooper, 1999), or an event perceived by some individuals as a reward or reinforcement, which, in contrast, may be perceived differently by others (Carrim, 2012), brought about this definition. Haine, Ayers, Sandler, Wolhick, and Weyer (2003) defined LOC as the self-system beliefs that people form about themselves and their collaborations with the social environment that in turn can be a source of distress or, on the contrary, act as a personal resource.

N. MH. Carrim et al., *Occupational Stress in South African Work Culture*, SpringerBriefs in Psychology, https://doi.org/10.1007/978-981-33-6397-7_5

5.2 Types of Locus of Control: Internal and External

Muhonen and Torkelson (2004) mention that it has been reported that LOC is one of the most-cited constructs and also that Rotter's I-E (internal-external) scale has been reported to be one of the most frequently used scales in various studies (Antonovsky, 1991; Furnham & Steele, 1993). Locus of control refers to "an individual's personal belief that the events which occur in life are either a result of personal control and effort, or outside forces such as fate or luck" (Graffeo & Silvestri, 2006, p. 593). According to Rotter (1966), a person's "locus" (Latin for "location" or "place") is hypothesised as either internal or external. Uguak, Elias, Uli, and Suandi (2001), argue that LOC can be defined as the location of control over our lives. In order to understand what the concept LOC as the root of the domain-specific WLOC measure encompasses, it is important to look at a variety of definitions that scholars have formulated in order to create one's own understanding of the concept.

Furthermore, studies indicate that an external locus of control is per definition associated with less favourable outcomes, for example, poor psychological or physical health (Scott, Carper, Middleton, White, & Renk, 2010). It can be assumed that poor psychological or physical health can in turn have a dire effect on an organisation's productivity.

Rodriguez, Bravo, Peiro, and Schaufeil (2001) argue that it is important to include LOC in occupational stress research. It can be used as a predictive indicator that an individual with an internal LOC will be expected to cope with stress more effectively. On the other hand, individuals with an external LOC will rather avoid such actions, because they believe that changing the situation is beyond their control span or ability (Van Niekerk, 2011).

Therefore, it is noted that externals tend to perceive more stressors (Muhonen & Torkelson, 2004) than their counterparts, and subsequently these individuals (externals) are likely to have lower job satisfaction and organisational commitment (Macan, Trusty, & Trimble, 1996; Spector, 1988). It is noted that WLOC is more predictive in relation to perceived stressors and job stress, amongst others, than general LOC (Tong & Wang, 2006).

Rotter (1966) described LOC as a personality variable that signifies the extent to which individuals perceive that they are in control of, or are controlled by, their environment. Thus, LOC as a personality variable has given rise to much of the historical controversy surrounding personality theory and research (Maram & Miller, 1998). According to Mohapatra and Gupta (2010) and Lefcourt (1976), LOC can be seen as an aspect of personality that reflects an individual's beliefs about who controls life and the environment. It is suggested that LOC can be seen as a personality trait that "measures an individual's expectancies for either the need for internal or external control of reinforcement" (Rotter, 1966, p. 2). LOC is observed to be related to numerous variables of personality, such as motivation, attitude and behaviour, and specifically to behaviour related to work, stress, job satisfaction and commitment to change (Chen & Wang, 2007; Erez & Judge, 2001; Muhonen & Torkelson, 2004).

Previous studies indicate that the relationship between personality, job satisfaction, job performance and occupational stress has intensively been examined. For example, Choo (1986) found the level of stress perceived by individuals is contingent upon their personality type. Furthermore, Spector and O'Connell (1994) found that an individual's personality type might be a determining factor in the decision of an individual to enter a job which is naturally inclined to have high stress levels. Rahim (1996) points out the believability of an individual with a high internal LOC to be able to cope with stress more effectively than another person with an external LOC. Kalbers and Fogarty (2005) provide evidence supporting the fact that externals are more prone to be susceptible to stress and are thus more likely to perceive the event as stressful.

To substantiate this definition given by Rotter (1966), the concept of LOC as explained in earlier studies is that when a person enters a particular situation, his or her possible behaviours is either internal or external in nature with regard to expectations concerning the most likely outcome of that behaviour (Ajzen, 2002; Rotter, 1975). According to Rotter (1966), these expectations derive from an individual's LOC, which can be either internal or external.

5.3 Locus of Control: Uni-Dimensional or Multi-dimensional

Levenson (1973) maintained that Rotter's internal-external (I-E) LOC scale is too broad a classification of an individual's centrality of control. Rotter theorised that individuals who perceive reinforcements as a result of their own behaviour are classified as internals, whereas those individuals who perceive reinforcements a direct result of fate, chance, or powerful others, are considered to be externals. Furthermore, Rotter (1966) maintained that individuals at the extreme ends of the I-E continuum are more likely to be maladjusted than those in the middle range. Levenson (1973) argued that Rotter's (1966) classification of externals is too broad. According to Rotter's (1966) classification, all individuals who believe that the outcomes of situations are determined by chance, luck, fate or powerful others are externals, without distinguishing between them.

In this regard, Levenson (1973, p. 261) took issue with this broad classification and maintained that "people who believe the world is unordered (chance) would behave and think differently from people who believe the world is ordered but that powerful others are in control. In the latter case a potential for control exists." This argument consequently led to Levenson developing a three-dimensional locus of control scale (internal, powerful others, and chance scale—IPC scale). This significant progress in better distinguishing between each individual's sources of external LOC expectancies has led to LOC being considered as a multidimensional construct, and not unidimensional, as initially perceived by Rotter (1966).

Muhonen and Torkelson (2004) stated that LOC can be observed as either a uni- or multidimensional construct. Uni-dimensionality can be described as a global control belief, whereas multidimensionality can be described as an indication of the fact that individuals may differ in regard to their LOC beliefs depending on the area of their lives (Hewitt & Flett, 1996). Pertaining to domain-specific measures, Muhonen and Torkelson (2004) argue that when using LOC as a domain-specific measure, as in the work context, the utilisation of LOC as a multidimensional construct is required.

5.4 Conceptualising the WLOC Construct

Locus of control is related to various individual attitudes and behaviours, such as performance (Erez & Judge, 2001) and job satisfaction (Muhonen & Torkelson, 2004). Given the fact that LOC is perceived to be a general measure which is based on the assumptions of stability and generality of the construct, both Rotter (1975) and Phares (1976) argued that the need exists to develop domain specific measures of LOC. In response to this need, researchers increasingly started to develop and adapt existing LOC measures for behaviours and domains that deemed to be worth predicting (Maram & Miller, 1998).

In this regard, WLOC is considered to be the domain-specific version of the more generally known LOC construct (Tong & Wang, 2006; Spector, 1988). In order to understand WLOC as a domain specific measure, it is necessary to have an initial understanding LOC as the root or foundation, of WLOC. Furthermore, it is important to be familiarised with the theoretical background of this domain-specific measure. In this regard, it is noted by Wolk and Bloom (1978, p. 279) that "one of the most intriguing, yet unresolved questions related to locus of control (as a personality determinant of behaviour) concerns the role of expectancy for control in an individual's reaction to threat and stress". It is noted that the use of domain-specific scales was suggested to measure the construct of LOC in organisational studies, in contrast to the use of the general I-E scale of Rotter (1966) (Lefcourt, 1992). Figure 5.1 is a visual illustration of how WLOC can be considered to be a domain-specific measure of locus of control. This figure was compiled by one of the authors based on the notion that an individual's work locus of control is directly derived from that person's likelihood to attribute his or her successes and failures to his or her own doings or to that of the environment.

WLOC is specifically focused on the work context and is mainly concerned with "organisational rewards or outcomes such as promotions, salary increases and general career advancement" (Maram & Miller, 1998, p. 48). Tong, Arora, White, and Nichols (2011, p. 203) stated that Rotter (1975) defined WLOC as "a domain-specific expectancy that rewards, reinforcements or outcomes are controlled either by one's own actions (internality) or by other forces (externality)". It is argued that this belief in personal control has a significant impact on both the experience of frustration as well as on the affective and behavioural responses to experienced frustration (Fox &

Fig. 5.1 Work locus of control as domain-specific measure of locus of control (*Source* Oosthuizen, 2016)

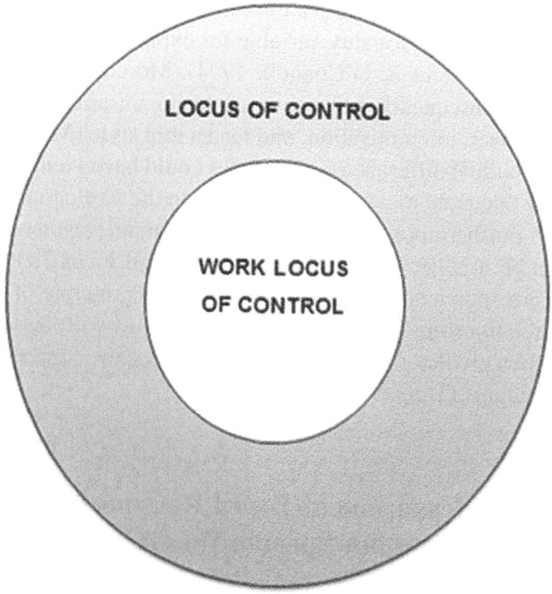

Spector, 1999). In this regard, it is postulated that individuals with an external LOC are more likely to perceive more stressors (Muhonen & Torkelson, 2004).

5.5 General Versus Domain-Specific Locus of Control

Various authors (Caton & Nowicki, 1997; Findley & Cooper, 1983; Kalechstein & Nowicki, 1997; Stipek & Weisz, 1981) have argued that the inherent characteristics of the LOC construct, specifically, the scales' specificity or generality pertaining to the behaviour measured, may facilitate the relationship between the specific behaviour and LOC orientation.

The LOC measure (Rotter, 1966) is considered as a global characteristic perceived to be stable across life domains. However, it is has been demonstrated that an individual displaying internally orientated behaviours in one situation would most probably display externally orientated behaviours in a different situation (Tong et al., 2011). Thus, on these premises Rotter (1975) also acknowledged that control orientations (internal orientation or external orientation) are so often situationally determined. This led to Rotter suggesting the development and use of a domain-specific measure. Since it has been reported that the construct LOC will change in different domains, it is anticipated that domain-specific LOC measures will be better predictors than generalised LOC measures of variables associated with their relevant domains (Tong et al., 2011).

Increasingly, more evidence indicates that WLOC is considered to be an important and useful personality variable for explaining behaviour in the work context (Blau, 1993; Spector & O'Connell, 1994). Moreover, it is reported that personal control may subsequently influence various organisational factors, such as job performance, turnover, job motivation, and leadership style (Macan, 1996). Based on the fact that individual differences in variables could have vital implications for the organisation, the adequate measurement of LOC in the work context is a key concern.

Furthermore, it is noted that another main reason why the WLOC has been reported to be a better predictor than the general locus LOC is based on the principle of correspondence (Tong et al., 2011). The principle of correspondence maintains that "relationships of attitudes and perceptions with behavioural outcomes are stronger when predictors and criteria refer to the same context, for example the specific work domain" (Tong et al., 2011, p. 203).

5.6 Measurement-Based Reasons for Use of Domain-Specific WLOC

Besides the above theoretical justification for the use of a WLOC measure, Tong et al. (2011) proposed that items derived from predictor and indicator measures in the same domain are likely to be more closely correlated than those from different domains. Based on this argument, Ang and Chang (1999) demonstrated that "domain-specific measures of locus of control are significant predictors of behaviour for respective domain-relevant goals but not for goals in the non-related realm" (Tong et al., 2011, p. 203).

5.7 Research on WLOC

Quite a bit of research was done the last twenty years using the WLOC measure. For example, Blakely, Srivastava, and Moorman (2005) conducted a study on a sample of 116 Chinese managers and 109 American managers and discovered that compared to their Chinese counterparts, American managers who held an internal locus of control saw Occupational Citizenship Behaviour as part of their jobs. Bosman and Buitendach (2005) conducted a study investigating the relationship between job insecurity, work locus of control and dispositional optimism of 603 employees of two financial institutions in Gauteng, South Africa. It was found that external work locus of control leads to an increase in job security, and internal work locus of control decrease job insecurity. König et al. (2010) examined whether three possible resources (occupational self-efficacy, work locus of control and communication) moderate the negative job insecurity-performance relationship. The sample consisted of 311 participants from a Swiss logistics company. The study indicated a relationship between WLOC and perceived communication with self-rated task performance. It was found that where job insecurity was low WLOC and perceived communication was related to self-rated task performance. The findings also found a relationship between WLOC, self-efficacy and perceived communication. It was found that resources locus of control and communication can only be beneficial in situations where job insecurity is low. The study indicated that the relationship between locus of control or communication with self-efficacy is affected by job insecurity. Sprung and Jex (2012) conducted a study aimed to determine whether work locus of control served as a moderator of the relationship between work stressors and counterproductive work behaviour. The results of the study indicated that interaction between work locus of control and work stressors account for 1–2% of the variance in counterproductive behaviour. Organisational constraints and interpersonal conflict were more strongly related to counterproductive behaviour of employees with an external WLOC, thus WLOC is an important variable to consider in counterproductive work behaviour studies. Wilski, Chmielewski, and Tomczak (2015) conducted a study was to explain the relationship between work locus of control and burnout in 155 Polish physiotherapists through the mediation of coping styles. The hypothesis of the study was partially confirmed as the relationship between external work locus of control and burnout was shown to be mediated by emotion- and problem-focused coping. The findings of the study indicate that part of the work locus of control-burnout symptoms association is mediated by coping practices. Van Niekerk (2011) had conducted research on 300 nurses from diverse hospitals within the South African context related to their Locus of control and job satisfaction. However, this research was based on Rotter's ipsative instrument where participants were forced to choose between one, or the other option, and were not provided flexibility in their choice of answers.

Although it has been noted that empirical evidence is limited regarding the use of WLOC as indicated in the studies above which mainly use the generalised LOC measures, the measuring of WLOC in the work context has been encouraged (Spector, 1988). On this basis, evidence as discussed in the preceding paragraphs indicates that the domain-specific WLOC scale is perceived to be a better predictor of work-related outcomes in comparison to its counterpart, the generalised LOC scale.

The work locus of control scale (WLCS) was developed by Spector in 1988 as a measure of generalised control beliefs in the work context (Spector, 1988). In this regard, Muhonen and Torkelson (2004) asserted that the WLCS is considered to be a domain-specific measure of LOC specifically concerning the work context. During the development of the WLCS, Spector used six independent and diverse samples: municipal managers; undergraduate students; mental health agency employees (two samples); convenience store employees; and, department store employees. Initially, the item pool of the WLCS scale consisted of 49 items. These 49 items were generated from a theoretical analysis of the LOC construct and the manner in which it related to work behaviour.

Three criteria were used in selecting the items included in the WLCS: (i) acceptable item-total correlations, (ii) lack of correlation with social desirability, and (iii) that the scale should have an equal number of internally and externally phrased items. Item-totals ranged from 0.24 to 0.67, with a mean inter-item correlation of

0.25. Coefficient alphas for all six samples ranged from 0.75 to 0.85. The internal consistency of the scale proves to be adequate. The final scale consists of 16 items, and uses response choices ranging from 1 = disagree very much to 6 = agree very much. Adhering to the criteria, the results obtained suggest that Spector's WLCS is a viable scale. Tong et al. (2011) assert that since the development of the WLCS, the measure has been employed in an extensive range of research, and that these studies provide solid, validated evidence.

In regard to LOC in the work context, Maram and Miller (1998) assert that Spector's WLCS is noted to be the only domain-specific measure of LOC used in the work setting. According to Rigotti, Schyns, and Mohr (2008), the WLCS can be described as a broad measure developed for the purposes of evaluating employees in organisations. The measure is designed in such a fashion that it focuses primarily on employees' beliefs about people in general, rather than their beliefs concerning themselves. Thus, on these premises it is postulated that reports about an employee's self would predict his or her attitudes and behaviours better than reports about people in general at work (Tong et al., 2011).

Furthermore, Spector (1988) undertook to validate the WLCS by drawing correlations between his measure and the work variables that had already been correlated against Rotter's (1966) scale. In this regard, it is noted that a number of studies (Blau, 1993; Cvetanovski & Jex, 1994; Spector, 1988) have reported that there is an overlap between Rotter's LOC measure and Spector's WLCS measure, with correlations ranging between 0.49 and 0.63. It is noted that Spector's findings suggested that the correlations between the WLCS and the work variables were significantly stronger than those correlations reported in terms of those same work variables and Rotter's more general LOC scale (Macan, 1996; Maram & Miller, 1998).

In the light of establishing whether the WLOC measure is more useful than the general LOC measure, it is cited that previous research found that the relationships between domain-specific LOC measures and criterion variables are stronger than those between general scales of LOC and criteria (Tong et al., 2011). However, Tong et al. (2011) point out that due to the fact that there was no significant test between the two correlations, the correlation comparison was not deemed as trustworthy.

Maram and Miller (1998) point out that not much subsequent research has been done which has used the WLOC scale to substantiate the validation as established by Spector (1988). However, it is noted that the studies of Orpen (1992), Blau (1993) and Macan (1996), suggest that the variable is worth investigating by concluding that the WLOC scale does indeed have stronger correlations to the work variables in comparison to that of the general LOC scale of Rotter (1966). Even though it has been maintained that WLOC is a better predictor of attitudes and behaviour in the work context, it is still reported that many of the LOC studies in organisational settings have not used the WLCS (Muhonen & Torkelson, 2004).

5.8 Theory Relevant to WLOC: Attribution Theory

Lefcourt's (1976) definition of LOC substantiates Ajzen's (2002) theory of planned behaviour. On these premises of expectancy, the theory of planned behaviour has become known as one of the most prominent and prevalent frameworks used to conceptualise human action. It is cited that human behaviour, according to the theory of planned behaviour, is guided by three types of considerations: "beliefs about the likely consequences or other attributes of the behaviour (behavioural beliefs), beliefs about the normative expectations of other people (normative beliefs), and beliefs about the presence of factors that may further or hinder performance of the behaviour (control beliefs)" (Ajzen, 2002, p. 665). These three viewpoints that people hold can in turn be used to understand why people attribute successes and failures either to internal control factors or to external control factors.

The first attribution theory was proposed by Heider, Jones, Davis, and Kelly in 1958 (Borkowski, 2010). The attribution theory is considered to be a cognitive approach to understanding human behaviour (Weiner, 1972). Borkowski noted that the work of Heider et al. suggests that individuals have two main behavioural motives, namely (i) the need to control their environment, and (ii) the need to understand the world around them. Furthermore, it is cited that the attribution theory describes "how an individual's perceived reasons for past success and failure contribute to their current and future motivation and success" (Assessing Women in Engineering, 2005, p. 1). On these premises, it is argued that the attribution theory deals with how individuals explain things that happen to them (Carrim, 2012). Carrim further maintains that there are two methods that can be used to explain why things happen, namely (i) an internal attribution, and (ii) an external attribution. An internal attribution implies that an individual is directly responsible for the outcome of an event (Carrim, 2012) while an external attribution assigns the cause to an external source or agent (Smith, 2003).

When describing the attribution theory at the hand of WLOC, it is noted that central differences in the achievement theory characterise individuals as high or low in their need for achievement, which in relation can be seen as individuals with an internal WLOC or an external WLOC (Atkinson, 1984). Previous research has identified a variable that measures variations in how individuals explain the factors that contribute to successes and failures; this variable is labelled attributional style (Graham, 1991). The study of Peterson and Seligman (1984) on attributional style, discovered that individuals explain failures by attributing the bad outcomes to personal characteristics that are established and comprehensive, to be prone to have feelings of helplessness and that they do not have control. These individuals are thought to have a pessimistic attributional style. On the contrary, individuals who attribute failure to external causes are seen to have an optimistic attributional style (Graham, 1991).

Pertaining to attribution styles, a study by Seel, Keith and Angelini (2004) provided evidence that different attribution styles are considered to be the basis from which one can characterise and explain why people react differently, but predictably, to events and also to the causes of an event. According to Park and Kim (1998), this occurrence can be explained by noting that individuals are likely to attribute success to personal ability or characteristics, and failure to a task; this phenomenon is considered to have a self-serving bias. Carrim (2012) noted that there are four main attributions that individuals tend to make, namely, (i) internal attributions about themselves when they are successful, (ii) internal attributions about others when they fail, (iii) external attributions about themselves when they fail, and (iv) external attributions about others when they succeed.

It is noted that people attempt to make sense of their realities by making attributions regarding the cause of certain outcomes (Heider in Shabazz, 2007). In his study, Heider points out that the causal element of certain outcomes can be divided into two categories, namely, personal and situational causes. In this regard, the term attributional style can be defined as the degree to which people utilise similar combinations of these causes over time (Assessing Women in Engineering, 2005). In this regard, Heider further states that one can distinguish between two types of attributional styles, namely (i) causal attribution, and (ii) self-enhancing attribution.

Causal attribution can be described as how individuals understand the reasons for their success and failure (Assessing Women in Engineering, 2005). According to the attribution theory, causal attribution exists along a continuum of three dimensions, namely (i) stable or unstable, (ii) internal and/or external, and (iii) controllable and/or uncontrollable. The stability dimension proposes that causes may change over time or they may not; for example, ability can be viewed as a stable aspect, while effort can be viewed as unstable (Weiner, 1985). Locus of control, and subsequently WLOC, has two distinctive continuums, namely (i) internal WLOC, and (ii) external WLOC. Lastly, the degree of controllability is related to the causes that individuals perceive to be under their control, such as skill, and the causes that they regard to be out of their control, emotions and moods.

Pertaining to causal attributions, Weiner (1985, 1995) maintains that individuals attribute event outcomes in achievement situations to one of four basic causes, namely (i) ability, (ii) effort, (iii) chance/luck, and (iv) difficulty of task. These four basic causes are derived from Weiner's (1979) proposed model that is based on the strongest elements of LOC. Weiner also stated that the LOC dimension in his model influenced individuals' feelings of pride (as in the result of success) and shame (as in the event of failure).

It is noted that Kivilu and Rogers (1997) support Weiner's model by concluding from their study that pride is enhanced when individuals ascribe their success to their own internal attributes (ability and effort), and decreased substantially when an individual saw success to be caused by external factors (task difficulty and luck). Furthermore, it is also noted that accordingly, emotions of shame increased when failure was due to internal qualities, and decreased when failure was due to external causes (Weiner, 1979).

On the other hand, self-enhancing attributional styles are regarded as more motivational than self-defeating attributional styles (Assessing Women in Engineering, 2005). In this regard, when individuals attribute the causes of their success to internal and controllable features, and the causes of failure to external and unstable factors, they are evidently enhancing themselves, given that this manner of thinking compels a person to incorporate positive outcomes to enhance self-concept, which in turn will eliminate the incorporation of negative outcomes (Kashima, Foddy, & Platow, 2002). Finally, Rotter suggested that individuals act in a particular way with an expectation from that behaviour, which is directly linked to a value of the result expected from that specific behaviour (Cüceloğlu, 1996).

The attribution theory serves as a theoretical basis for understanding the impact that an individual's emotions and behaviour subsequently have on that individual's expectations. However, it is important to take note of the limitations that are associated with the attribution theory, namely (i) the initial development of the theory was developed on the basis of a universal theory of human sense-making, but further research has addressed this limitation by limiting its scope; (ii) the attribution theory, to some extent, may be limited by cultural restraints; and (iii) in contexts where the importance of making an attribution is less necessary, the attributions may or may not work.

5.9 Summary of Chapter 5

The concept of work locus of control (as introduced in Chapter 1), was more elaborated on in this chapter. The history of work locus of control was discussed, in which the change from research on general locus of control only towards the workplace place, and its impact on health was further debated. The concepts of internal and external locus of control were discussed by assessing it from the Attribution theory perspective, where the notion of effort and ability vs external stimuli were found to be dependent on the organisational and the type of job. In the next chapter, the relationship between occupational stress and work locus of control will be explored.

References

Ajzen, I. (2002). Perceived behavioural control, self-efficacy, locus of control, and the theory of planned behaviour. *Journal of Applied Social Psychology, 32,* 665–683.

Ang, R. P., & Chang, W. C. (1999). Impact of domain-specific locus of control on need for achievement and affiliation. *The Journal of Social Psychology, 139,* 527–529.

Antonovsky, A. (1991). The structural sources of salutogenic strengths. In C. L. Cooper & R. Payne (Eds.), *Personality and stress: Individual differences in the stress process.* Chichester, UK: Wiley.

Assessing Women in Engineering (AWE) Project. (2005). *Attribution theory.* Retrieved August 15, 2014, from, Assessing Woman and Men in Engineering Web site: http://www.aweonline.org.

Atkinson, J. (1984). Manpower strategies for flexible organisations. *Personnel Management, 16,* 28–31.

Blakely, G. L., Srivastava, A., & Moorman, R. H. (2005). The effects of nationality work role centrality, and work locus of control on role definitions of OCB. *Journal of Leadership & Organizational Studies, 12*(1), 103–117.

Blau, G. (1993). Testing the relationship of locus of control to different performance dimensions. *Journal of Occupational and Organizational Psychology, 66,* 125–138.
Borkowski, N. (2010). *Organizational behaviour in health care* (2nd ed.). Sudbury, MA: Jones and Bartlett.
Bosman, J., & Buitendach, J. H. (2005). Work locus of control and dispositional optimism as antecedents to job insecurity. *SA Journal of Industrial Psychology, 31*(4), 17–23.
Carrim, N. M. H. (2012). *The relationship amongst locus of control, self-determination and job satisfaction in call centres.* Unpublished master's thesis. University of Pretoria, Pretoria, South Africa.
Caton, J. S., & Nowicki, S. (1997). Antecedents of individual differences in locus of control of reinforcement: A critical review. *Genetic, Social, and General Psychology Monographs, 120,* 31–81.
Chen, J., & Wang, L. (2007). Locus of control and the three components of commitment to change. *Personality and Individual Differences, 42,* 503–512.
Choo, F. (1986). Job stress, job performance, and auditor personality characteristics. *Auditing: A Journal of Practice and Theory, 5*(2), 17–34.
Cüceloğlu, D. (1996). *İnsan ve davranışı.* İstanbul, Turkey: Remzi Kitabevi.
Cvetanovski, J., & Jex, S. M. (1994). Locus of control of unemployed people and its relationship to psychological and physical well-being. *Work & Stress, 8,* 60–67.
Erez, A., & Judge, T. A. (2001). Relationship of core self-evaluations to goal setting, motivation, and performance. *Journal of Applied Psychology, 86,* 1270–1279.
Findley, M. J., & Cooper, H. M. (1983). Locus of control and academic achievement: A literature review. *Journal of Personality and Social Psychology, 4*(2), 419–427.
Fox, S., & Spector, P. E. (1999). A model of work frustration–aggression. *Journal of Organizational Behavior, 20,* 915–931.
Furnham, A., & Steele, H. (1993). Measuring locus of control: a critique of general, children's, health- and work-related locus of control questionnaires. *British Journal of Psychology, 84,* 443–479.
Graffeo, L. C., & Silvestri, L. (2006). Relationship between locus of control and health-related variables. *Education, 126*(3), 593–596.
Graham, J. W. (1991). An essay on organizational citizenship behavior. *Employee Responsibilities and Rights Journal, 4,* 249–270.
Haine, R. A., Ayers, T. S., Sandler, I. A., Wolchick, S. A., & Weyer, J. L. (2003). Locus of control and self-esteem as stress-moderators or stress-mediators in parentally bereaved children. *Death Studies, 27*(7), 619–641.
Hewitt, P. L., & Flett, G. (1996). Personality traits and the coping process. In M. Zeidner & N. S. Endler (Eds.), *Handbook of coping: Theory, research, applications* (pp. 410–433). New York, NY: Wiley.
Kalbers, L. P., & Fogarty, T. J. (2005). Antecedents to internal auditor burnout. *Journal of Managerial Issues, 1,* 101–118.
Kalechstein, A. D., & Nowicki, S. (1997). A meta-analytic examination of the relationship between control expectancies and academic achievement: An 11-year follow-up to Findley and Cooper. *Genetic, Social, and General Psychology Monographs, 123*(1), 27–56.
Kashima, Y., Foddy, M., & Platow, M. J. (2002). *Self and identity: Personal, social, and symbolic.* Mahwah, NJ: Lawrence Erlbaum.
Kivilu, J. M., & Rogers, W. T. (1997). A multi-level analysis of cultural experience and gender influences on causal attributions to perceived performance in mathematics. *International Development Research Centre (IDRC), 68,* 25–37.
König, C. J., Debus, M. E., Häusler, S., Lendenmann, N., & Kleinmann, M. (2010). Examining occupational self-efficacy, work locus of control and communication as moderators of the job insecurity—Job performance relationship. *Economic and Industrial Democracy, 31*(2), 231–247.
Lefcourt, H. M. (1976). *The locus of control: Current trends in theory and research.* New York, NY: Wiley.

Lefcourt, H. M. (1992). Durability and impact of the locus of control construct. *Psychological Bulletin, 112,* 411–414.

Levenson, H. (1973). Multidimensational locus of control in psychiatric patients. *Journal of Consulting and Clinical Psychology, 41,* 397–404.

Lu, L., Wu, H., & Cooper, C. L. (1999). Perceived work stress and locus of control: A combined quantitative and qualitative approach. *Research and Practice in Human Resource Management, 7*(1), 1–15.

Macan, T. H. (1996). Time-management training: Effects on time behaviors, attitudes, and job performance. *The Journal of psychology, 130*(3), 229–236.

Maram, A., & Miller, K. (1998). An empirical assessment of the construct work locus of control. *Journal of Industrial Psychology, 24*(3), 48–51.

Mohapatra, M., & Gupta, A. (2010). Relationship of emotional intelligence with work values & internal locus of control: A study of managers in a public sector organization. *Vilakshan: XIMB Journal of Management, 7*(2), 1–20.

Muhonen, T., & Torkelson, E. (2004). Work locus of control and its relationship to health and job satisfaction from a gender perspective. *Stress and Health, 20,* 21–28.

Oosthuizen, M. M. (2016). *The relationship between occupational stress and work locus of control amongst South African management: An exploratory study.* Unpublished M.Com. dissertation. University of Pretoria, Pretoria, South Africa.

Orpen, C. (1992). The work locus of control scale as a predictor of employee attitudes and behaviour: A validity study. *Journal of Human Behavior, 2,* 35–37.

Park, Y. S., & Kim, U. (1998). Locus of control, attributional style, and academic achievement: Comparative analysis of Korean, Korean-Chinese, and Chinese students. *Asian Journal of Social Psychology, 1*(2), 191–208.

Peterson, C., & Seligman, M. E. (1984). Causal explanations as a risk factor for depression: Theory and evidence. *Psychological Review, 91*(3), 347–374.

Phares, E. J. (1976). *Locus of control in personality.* Morristown, NJ: General Learning Press.

Rahim, A. (1996). Stress, strain, and their moderators: An empirical comparison of entrepreneurs and managers. *Journal of Small Business Management, 34,* 46–58.

Rigotti, T., Schyns, B., & Mohr, G. (2008). A short version of the occupational self-efficacy scale: Structural and construct validity across five countries. *Journal of Career Assessment, 16,* 238–255.

Rodriguez, I., Bravo, M. J., Peiro, J. M., & Schaufeli, W. (2001). The demands-control-support model, locus of control and job satisfaction: A longitudinal study. *Work and Stress, 15*(2), 97–114.

Rotter, J. B. (1966). Generalised expectancies for internal versus external control of reinforcement. *Psychological Monographs, 80*(1), 169–214.

Rotter, J. B. (1975). Some problems and misconceptions related to the construct of internal versus external control of reinforcement. *Journal of Clinical and Consulting Psychology, 43,* 56–67.

Scott, S. L., Carper, T. M., Middleton, M., White, R., & Renk, K. (2010). Relationship among locus of control, coping behaviours, and level of worry following exposure to hurricanes. *Journal of Loss and Trauma, 15*(2), 123–137.

Seel, K., & Angelini, A. (2004, November). *Strengthening the capacity of executive directors.* Paper presented at the Association for Research on Nonprofit and Voluntary Action, Los Angeles.

Shabazz, K. M. (2007). *The effects of environment and age on locus of control, self-efficacy, and self-esteem of military and non-military students' academic achievement.* Unpublished doctoral thesis. Touro University International, Cypress, CA, USA.

Smith, V. L. (2003). *Analysis of locus of control and educational level utilizing the internal control index.* Unpublished master's dissertation. The Graduate College of Marshall University, Marshall University, Huntington, England.

Spector, P. E. (1988). Development of the Work locus of control scale. *Journal of Occupational Psychology, 61,* 335–340.

Spector, P., & O'Connell, B. J. (1994). The contribution of personality traits, negative, locus of control and Type A to the subsequent reports of job stressor and job strains. *Journal of Occupational and Organisational Psychology, 67*(1), 1–11.

Sprung, J. M., & Jex, S. M. (2012). Work locus of control as a moderator of the relationship between work stressors and counterproductive work behavior. *International Journal of Stress Management, 19*(4), 272–281.

Stipek, D. J., & Weisz, J. R. (1981). Perceived personal control and academic achievement. *Review of Education, 51,* 101–137.

Tong, M., Arora, K., White, M. M., & Nichols, R. A. (2011). Role of key aromatic residues in the ligand-binding domain of α7 nicotinic receptors in the agonist action of β-amyloid. *Journal of Biological Chemistry, 286*(39), 34373–34381.

Tong, J., & Wang, L. (2006). Validation of locus of control scale in Chinese organizations. *Personality and Individual Differences, 41,* 941–950.

Uguak, U. A., Elias, H. B., Uli, J., & Suandi, T. (2001). The influence of causal elements of locus of control on academic achievement satisfaction. *Journal of Instructional Psychology, 34*(2), 121–128.

Van Niekerk, M. (2011). The relationship between occupational stress and locus of control among nurses. Unpublished master's dissertation. University of Pretoria, Pretoria, South Africa.

Weiner, B. (1972). *Theories of motivation: From mechanism to cognition.* Chicago, IL: Markham.

Weiner, B. (1979). A theory of motivation for some classroom experiences. *Journal of Education, 71,* 3–25.

Weiner, B. (1985). An attributional theory of achievement motivation and emotion. *Psychological Review, 92,* 548–573.

Weiner, B. (1995). *Judgments of responsibility: A foundation for a theory of social conduct.* New York, NY: Guilford Press.

Wilski, M., Chmielewski, B., & Tomczak, M. (2015). Work locus of control and burnout in Polish physiotherapists: The mediating effect of coping styles. *International journal of occupational medicine and environmental health, 28*(5), 875.

Wolk, S., & Bloom, D. (1978). *The interactive effects of locus of control and situational stress upon performance accuracy and time.* Retrieved April 5, 2014, from http://interruptions.net/literature/Wolk-JP78.pdf.

Chapter 6
The Relationship Between Occupational Stress and Work Locus of Control for Managers

Abstract In this chapter, occupational stress and work locus of control are explored collectively. This provides the opportunity to jointly explore the factors that causes and lead to both occupational stress and work locus of control, and to provide theoretical and empirical evidence in how work locus of control impacts occupational stress.

Keywords Internal work locus of control · External locus of control · Stressors · Well-being · Organisational outcomes

6.1 Stressors of Occupational Stress and Work Locus of Control

Various stressors are evident that provide a holistic view of how occupational stress and work locus of control are formed and how they influence other factors in organisations. More specifically, it was clear that employees with different levels of work locus of control tend to prefer certain work conditions and stipulations. When these conditions are not met, if may influence occupational stress and have dire consequences for reaching organisational goals. This is further explored in this section, and how internal and external locus of control generally impacts on occupational stress and other work conditions before the relationships between the concepts are further explored in subsequent sections.

For instance, Oosthuizen (2016) found that individuals with an internal work locus of control (WLOC) prefer a high level of autonomy in performing their work tasks, whereas individuals with an external WLOC prefer a low level of autonomy in performing these tasks. Accordingly, individuals with an internal WLOC who sufficient authority in do not have performing their work tasks would experience frustration and role conflict, which will ultimately increase their levels of occupational stress. Conversely, individuals who have an external WLOC will perceive a significant increase in occupational stress if they are expected to exercise a high level of autonomy in the execution of their tasks. In this regard, WLOC and autonomy of work have a direct impact on employees' organisational commitment (Aubé, Rosseau, & Morin, 2007). It is noted that the less individuals have authority in the

N. MH. Carrim et al., *Occupational Stress in South African Work Culture*, SpringerBriefs in Psychology, https://doi.org/10.1007/978-981-33-6397-7_6

execution of their tasks, the more dependent they are on their employer (Semmer, 2000).

The results of the study by Oosthuizen (2016) indicates that autonomy in decision-making increases the participants' levels of occupational stress. The main reason for this increase in elevated stress levels is due to the fact that at managerial level, decisions made have a direct impact on the organisation's viability and, by extension, on the individual's job security. Various studies provide evidence of consistent positive relationships between intrinsically rewarding work and individual outcomes such as job satisfaction (see Malik & Dhar, 2017). Sufficient evidence also exists that, by extension, autonomy in decision-making directly translates into an increased ability for employees to control decisions, hence where and how to establish and maintain their work-life balance.

With respect to conflict handling, it was found that conflict in the workplace is not necessarily a negative occurrence, but can also add value to the performance of an organisation. Consistent with the study conducted by Oosthuizen (2016), it was found that participants mostly perceived conflict as constructive as it is regarded as necessary to increase performance. The argument of increased performance stems from the notion that conflict is the platform where individuals from different backgrounds bring their contributions to the table to find an optimal solution to a problem. However, the present study also found that if conflict goes unresolved, it will increase an individual's occupational stress. This finding is also supported by the literature in that performance has been found to increase as a result of conflict only to a certain level, and thereafter it declines if the conflict remains unresolved (Oosthuizen, 2016).

The origins of job stress are depicted as job stressors. In identifying the job stressors that cause the highest level of occupational stress, the researcher split the findings into two main job stressors, namely (i) stressors originating outside of the work environment and (ii) stressors arising from within the work environment. Catellano and Plionis (2006) argue that both of these categories should be evaluated to obtain a comprehensive understanding of the job stressors in the individuals' work environment.

Oosthuizen (2016) found that various stressors have an impact on the participants external to their working environment. It was noted that a spill-over effect (conflicting demands between job and family) exists between the participants' job stressors that are external and internal to the work situation. In this regard, the participants in this study experience an inter-role stress that is caused by their inability to meet the demands of both the work and the family domains. Robinson (2017) argue that inter-role conflict can originate from either an individual's work and/or family domain, hence the rationale for drawing a distinction between work-to-family conflict and family-to-work conflict. According to Robinson (2017), family-to-work conflict manifests when the individual experiences strain in fulfilling his or her work role due to participation in his or her family role. It was found that the participants in the current study are able to maintain a balance between their work and family responsibilities. However, they did indicate that they would experience inter-role stress should a dire event take place in their personal lives. It was also found that some managers experience inter-role conflict because the inherent nature of their role as manager stereotypically requires of them to be solely dedicated to their careers.

Furthermore, other aspects outside of the working environment that influence employees' stress levels are their health and specific life stage. In the present study, it was found that health-related issues increase occupational stress levels as they could potentially impede an employee's ability to perform his or her tasks optimally. With regards to life stage, it was found that an employee's life stage could potentially increase or decrease the levels of stress experienced by that person. The participants generally indicated that the responsibility of having children has an impact on their career aspirations, which in turn increases their occupational stress levels as their counterparts that do not have children progress in their careers at a far more rapid pace. By contrast, well-seasoned managers indicated that they view their life stage as an advantage as they have enough experience and knowledge to be at ease and confident in the execution of their tasks.

The work environment of managers poses inherently unique challenges. It was found that the most prominent of these challenges is related to recognition for a job well done. It was found that the individuals feel that they should be paid according to their skills and contribution, although employees value both verbal and monetary recognition. It has accordingly been argued that the relationship between remuneration and labour productivity is stronger when employees are highly skilled, such as managerial employees (Turner & Jackson, 2009).

In the next section, Oosthuizen's (2016) study will form the basis to discuss the relationship between occupational stress and WLOC.

6.2 Relationship Between Occupational Stress and Work Locus of Control

6.2.1 Internal Locus of Control and Occupational Stress

In the study by Oosthuizen (2016) a relationship between occupational stress and work locus of control was found. More specifically, it was found that an individual's work expectations and work experiences, respectively, are predictors of an individual's inclination towards an internal WLOC as these domains allow internals to control the outcomes by means of their actions and efforts. Work circumstances do not predict internal WLOC independently as internals have control over their work circumstances only to a certain extent, regardless of their efforts to control their immediate work environments. However, the researcher noted that all three stressor variables do predict internal WLOC when considered holistically. The researcher argues that the rationale for these findings is that individuals with an internal WLOC cope more effectively with job stressors. Studies conducted on managers confirm this finding by concluding that internals believe that they have the ability to cope with job stressors effectively (Rahim, 1996), whereas externals are more likely to be more vulnerable to occupational stress (Kalbers & Fogarty, 2005). The findings are concurrent with empirical evidence that suggests that the work locus of control-related personality traits can be linked to occupational stress (Sadri, Marcoulides, Cooper, & Kirkcaldy, 1996).

6.2.2 *External Locus of Control and Occupational Stress*

Oosthuizen (2016) further explored the relationship of occupational stress and work locus of control, and found that occupational stress does not predict an individual's inclination to have an external WLOC independently. However, when stressors from work expectations, work circumstances and experience of work are encountered simultaneously, it was found that the external WLOC can be predicted. This finding is concurrent with research in that external stressors independently do not have a significant impact on externals as these individuals are characterised for attributing their successes and failures to external forces (Tong & Wang, 2006). Therefore, an increase in each of the stressor domains measured independently is not sufficient cause for externals to be concerned about their work environment. However, an increase in the three stressor domains simultaneously, results in a stronger positive impact as these stressors can lead to ambiguity which translates into tension for externals but not for internals (Keenan & McBain, 1979).

The researcher is of the opinion that occupational stress is not a reliable predictor of an individual's inclination towards an external LOC as these individuals do not have an awareness of dysfunction as an outcome of perceived conditions in their work environment because they attribute their success and failures to external factors. In this regard, empirical research provides evidence that the level of occupational stress perceived by an individual is a function of his or her personality type (Choo, 1986). Spector and O'Connell (1994) argue that WLOC is considered to be a personality trait.

6.3 Summary of Chapter 6

This chapter discussed the relationship between occupational stress and work locus of control, more specifically focusing on their respective dimensions. It was found that most dimensions of occupational stress have a relationship with internal locus of control, while little evidence of a relationship between occupational stress and external locus of control was found. In the next chapter, the conclusions of the book will be discussed.

References

Aubé, C., Rousseau, V., & Morin, E. M. (2007). Perceived organizational support and organizational commitment: The moderating effect of locus of control and work autonomy. *Journal of Managerial Psychology, 22,* 479–495.

Catellano, C., & Plionis, E. (2006). Comparative analysis of three crisis intervention models applied to law enforcement first responders during 9/11 and hurricane Katrina. *Brief Treatment and Crisis Intervention, 6*(4), 326.

Choo, F. (1986). Job stress, job performance, and auditor personality characteristics. *Auditing: A Journal of Practice and Theory, 5*(2), 17–34.

Kalbers, L. P., & Fogarty, T. J. (2005). Antecedents to internal auditor burnout. *Journal of Managerial Issues, 1,* 101–118.

Keenan, A., & McBain, G. D. M. (1979). Effects of type A behavior, intolerance of ambiguity, and locus of control on the relationship between role stress and work-related outcomes. *Journal of Occupational Psychology, 52*(4), 277–285.

Malik, N., & Dhar, R. L. (2017). Authentic leadership and its impact on extra role behaviour of nurses. *Personnel Review, 46*(2), 277–296.

Oosthuizen, M. M. (2016). *The relationship between occupational stress and Work Locus of Control amongst South African management: An exploratory study.* Unpublished MCom dissertation, University of Pretoria, Pretoria, South Africa.

Rahim, A. (1996). Stress, strain, and their moderators: An empirical comparison of entrepreneurs and managers. *Journal of Small Business Management, 34,* 46–58.

Robinson, L. D. (2017). *The work-family interface and burnout in sole and partnered working Australian mothers.* Published doctoral thesis. University of Wollongong, Australia. Retrieved from https://ro.uow.edu.au/theses1/69.

Sadri, G., Marcoulides, G. A., Cooper, C. L., & Kirkcaldy, B. (1996). Testing a model of occupational stress across different countries. *Journal of Business and Manageement, 20,* 10–29.

Semmer, N. K. (2000). Control at work: Issues of specificity, generality, and legitimacy. In P. J. Walter & A. Grob (Eds.), *Control of human behavior, mental processes, and consciousness: Essays in honor of the 60th birthday of August Flammer* (pp. 555–564). Mahwah, NJ: Lawrence Erlbaum Associates.

Spector, P., & O'Connell, B. J. (1994). The contribution of personality traits, negative, locus of control and Type A to the subsequent reports of job stressor and job strains. *Journal of Occupational and Organisational Psychology, 67*(1), 1–11.

Tong, J., & Wang, L. (2006). Validation of locus of control scale in Chinese organizations. *Personality and Individual Differences, 41,* 941–950.

Turner, H. A., & Jackson, D. A. (2009). On the stability of wage differences and productivity-based wage policies: An international analysis. *British Journal of Industrial Relations, 7*(1), 1–18.

Chapter 7
Concluding Remarks and Implications for Managers and Organisations

Abstract In this chapter, further inferences are made towards occupational stress and work locus of control, and the consequences they have on managers and organisations. It was clear that managers with a strong internal work locus of control are prone to experience occupational stress more heavily than managers with a strong external work locus of control. However, individuals with a higher internal locus of control may be more able to manage stressors in their environment. Importantly, continuous levels of occupational stress have severe organisational consequences, like absenteeism, turnover and poor performance amongst others. Therefore, the management of occupational stress and understanding their impact pertaining to managers with different levels of work of control, are paramount for organisations to provide the necessary interventions to overcome these issues.

Keywords Organisational stressors · Individual stressors · Internal work locus of control · External locus of control · Occupational stress · Practical implications

7.1 Concluding Remarks of Occupational Stress and Work Locus of Control

In this book various elements of occupational stress and work locus of control were explored. Individuals with an internal LOC cope better with the stressor variables in their work environment as opposed to their external counterparts. Siu, Spector, Cooper, Lu, & Yu (2002) also confirmed that internal WLOC is related to a lowered perception of occupational stress and that an internal orientation to work control is considered as a moderator of the stress-strain relationship, as postulated by Rahim (1996). Occupational stress could be a predictor of an individual's WLOC orientation, given that the environment controls the stressors.

Internals perceive greater occupational stress levels because they take responsibility for the consequences of their actions and they more effectively manage these stress levels. Internals experience role conflict because of competing demands in their professional and personal lives; this appears to be due to their inability to be fully in control of the outcomes in both domains simultaneously. Because of the COVID-19 crisis, where remote work is the order of day, an inference may be made

N. MH. Carrim et al., *Occupational Stress in South African Work Culture*, SpringerBriefs in Psychology, https://doi.org/10.1007/978-981-33-6397-7_7

that individuals with a strong internal locus of control will struggle to juggle the merged work-life conditions.

Younger managers experience higher levels of occupational stress as a result of their expectations of their work environment. This finding is ascribed to the fact that more experienced managers have more realistic expectations of their roles and have learned over the years how to better manage these expectations.

7.2 Implications for Managers and Organisations

One practical implication is that occupational stress and the inability to deal with it effectively have been proven as one of the main causes of staff turnover. Hence, due to the inherent impact of managerial employees on business performance and the disruption that turnover in these types of positions could cause for organisations, it is ever more crucial for organisations to implement efforts toward looking after the physical and psychological well-being of their managers. In understanding individuals' WLOC orientation, organisations would be able to provide greater customised support in assisting their managers to effectively deal with the stressors that are specific to their roles.

As the economy is hit hard by COVID-19, and becomes increasingly more competitive, and work is becoming merged with personal life and fast-paced, organisations have to implement measures to ensure the well-being of employees and in so doing retain their services. Occupational stress has evolved to such an extent over the past few years that it has become a serious threat to employees' well-being (Liu, Spector, & Shi, 2007) and are even now more important than before.

The extent to which managerial employees perceive occupational stress is directly linked to their WLOC orientation. The key contribution of this book is to enable organisations to retain their key personnel, namely their managerial employees, by better understanding the factors that influence the manner in which they perceive occupational stress as determined by their WLOC orientation. How your employees experience the COVID-19 crisis can also be linked with their WLOC orientation, which may influence their work outcomes.

References

Ackfeldt, A., & Malhotra, N. (2013). Revisiting the role stress-commitment relationship: Can managerial interventions help? *European Journal of Marketing, 47*(3), 1–37.

Adenuga, O. A. (2015). Impact of occupational stress on job satisfaction and mental health of first bank employees: Implication for personnel psychologists. *Science, 1*(1), 15–21.

Adriaenssens, J., De Gucht, V., & Maes, S. (2015). Causes and consequences of occupational stress in emergency nurses, a longitudinal study. *Journal of Nursing Management, 23*(3), 346–358.

Adriaenssens, J., De Gucht, V., Van Der Doef, M., & Maes, S. (2011). Exploring the burden of emergency care: Predictors of stress-health outcomes in emergency nurses. *Journal of Advanced Nursing, 67*(6), 1317–1328.

African News Agency (ANA). (2018, April 24). *Work-related sickness costs SA billions of rands.* Retrieved from https://citizen.co.za/news/southafrica/1905408/work-related-sickness-costs-sa-billions-of-rands/.

Ajzen, I. (2002). Perceived behavioural control, self-efficacy, locus of control, and the theory of planned behaviour. *Journal of Applied Social Psychology, 32,* 665–683.

Ajzen, I., & Fishbein, M. (1977). Attitude—Behavior relationships: A theoretical analysis and review of empirical research. *Psychological Bulletin, 84,* 888–918.

Akanji, B. (2013). Occupational stress: A review on conceptualisations, causes and cure. *Economic Insights, 2*(3), 73–80.

Alawiye, A. (Nigerian eye, 5th February, 2014). *Bank workers live in fear as job losses continue.* Available at: http://www.nigerianeye.com/2014/02/bank-workerslive-inear-as-job-losses.losses.html.

Ang, R. P., & Chang, W. C. (1999). Impact of domain-specific locus of control on need for achievement and affiliation. *The Journal of Social Psychology, 139,* 527–529.

Antonovsky, A. (1991). The structural sources of salutogenic strengths. In C. L. Cooper & R. Payne (Eds.), *Personality and stress: Individual differences in the stress process.* Chichester, UK: Wiley.

April, K. A., Dharani, B., & Peters, K. (2012). Impact of locus of control expectancy on level of well-being. *Review of European Studies, 4*(2), 124–137.

Arnold, J., Cooper, C., & Robertson, T. (1995). *Work psychology* (2nd ed.). London, UK: Pitman.

Arshadi, N., & Damiri, H. (2013). The relationship of job stress with turnover intention and job performance: Moderating role of OBSE. *Procedia-Social and Behavioral Sciences, 84,* 706–710.

Ashong, G. G. N. A., Rogers, H., Botwe, B. O., & Anim-Sampong, S. (2016). Effects of occupational stress and coping mechanisms adopted by radiographers in Ghana. *Radiography, 22*(2), 112–117.

Assessing Women in Engineering (AWE) Project. (2005). *Attribution theory.* Retrieved August 15, 2014, from Assessing Woman and Men in Engineering Web site: http://www.aweonline.org.

Atkinson, J. (1984). Manpower strategies for flexible organisations. *Personnel Management, 16,* 28–31.

Aubé, C., Rousseau, V., & Morin, E. M. (2007). Perceived organizational support and organizational commitment: The moderating effect of locus of control and work autonomy. *Journal of Managerial Psychology, 22,* 479–495.

Azeez, R. O., & Adenuga, O. A. (2009). Effects of perceived stress, self-efficacy and mental health on psychological well-being of secondary school teachers. *The Educational Psychologists, 7,* 144–152.

Babbie, E. (2007). *The practice of social research* (11th ed.). Belmont, CA: Thomson Wadsworth.

Bandura, A. (1997). *Self-efficacy: The exercise of control.* New York, NY: Freeman.

Baum, A., Trevino, L. A., & Dougall, A. L. (2011). Stress and the cancers. In R. J. Contrada & R. J. Baum (Eds.), *The handbook of stress science: Biology, psychology, and health* (pp. 411–424). New York, NY, USA: Springer Publishing Company, LLC.

BauNews. (2010). *South Africa's new mining charter.* Retrieved September 9, 2014, from http://www.southafrica.info/business/economy/policies/miningcharter-140910.htm#.VA82m_nohSk#ixzz3Cq94SKRH.

Beehr, T. A. (1995). *Psychological stress in the workplace.* London, UK: Routledge.

Beehr, T. A., & Newman, J. E. (1978). Job stress, employee health, and organizational effectiveness: A facet analysis, model, and literature review. *Personnel Psychology, 31,* 665–699.

Beheshtifar, M., Mohammad-Rafiei, R., & Nekoie-Moghadam, M. (2013). The investigation of relation between occupational stress and career plateau. *Interdisciplinary Journal of Contemporary Research in Business, 4*(11), 650–660.

Bennett, J. (2000). SA's unfulfilled potential. *Sunday Times,* July 9.

Berry, A., & Otley, D. (2004). Case-based research in accounting. In C. Humprey & B. Lee (Eds.), *The real-life guide to accounting research: A behind-the-scenes view of using qualitative research methods* (pp. 231–255). New York, NY: Elsevier.

Bhagat, R. S., & Beehr, T. A. (1985). An evaluation summary and recommendations for future research. In T. A. Beehr & R. S. Bhagat (Eds.), *Human stress and cognition in organization: An integrated perspective.* New York: Wiley.

Bhagat, R. S., Ford, D. L., O'Driscoll, M. P., Frey, L., Babakus, E., & Mahanyele, M. (2001). Do South African managers cope differently from American managers? A cross-cultural investigation. *International Journal of Intercultural Relations, 25,* 301–313.

Blakely, G. L., Srivastava, A., & Moorman, R. H. (2005). The effects of nationality work role centrality, and work locus of control on role definitions of OCB. *Journal of Leadership & Organizational Studies, 12*(1), 103–117.

Blau, G. (1993). Testing the relationship of locus of control to different performance dimensions. *Journal of Occupational and Organizational Psychology, 66,* 125–138.

Bless, C., & Higson-Smith, Q. (1995). *Fundamentals of social research methods: An African perspective.* Cape Town: Creda Press.

Bloomberg. (2012). *South African mines strike to cut exports by 12.5 Billion Rand.* Retrieved September 3, 2014, from http://www.bloomberg.com/news/2012-11-06/south-african-mine-strikes-to-cut-exports-by-12-5-billion-rand.html.

Bloomberg Day. (2013). *Chamber of mines warns on electricity increases.* Retrieved August 19, 2014, from http://www.capetownpc.org.za/docs/speeches/Challenges-facing-the-South-African-mining-industry-Comments-by-Peter-Leon-to-the-Cape-Town-Press.pdf.

Blunch, N. J. (2008). *Introduction to structural equation modelling using SPSS and AMOS.* London, UK: Sage. http://0-dx.doi.org.innopac.up.ac.za/10.4135/9781446249345.

Bond, F. W., & Bunce, D. (2003). The role of acceptance and job control in mental health, job satisfaction, and work performance. *Journal of Applied Psychology, 88*(6), 1057–1067.

Booysen, L. (2007). Barriers to employment equity implementation and retention of blacks in management in South Africa. *South African Journal of Labour Relations, 31*(1), 47–71.

Borkowski, N. (2010). *Organizational behaviour in health care* (2nd ed.). Sudbury, MA: Jones and Bartlett.

Bosman, J., & Buitendach, J. H. (2005). Work locus of control and dispositional optimism as antecedents to job insecurity. *SA Journal of Industrial Psychology, 31*(4), 17–23.

Botha, C., & Pienaar, J. (2006). South African correctional official occupational stress: The role of psychological strengths. *Journal of Criminal Justice, 34*(1), 73–84.

Boyatzis, R. E. (1998). *Transforming qualitative information.* Cleveland: Sage.

Branham, L. (2005). Planning to become an employer of choice. *Journal of Organizational Excellence, 24*(3), 57–68.

Braun, V., & Clarke, V. (2006). Using thematic analysis in psychology. *Qualitative Research in Psychology, 3,* 77–101.

Broom, A. (2005). Using qualitative interviews in CAM research: A guide to study design, data collection and data analysis. *Complementary Therapies in Medicine, 13*(1), 65–73. https://doi.org/10.1016/j.ctim.2005.01.001.

Bryman, A., & Bell, E. (2007). *Business research methods* (2nd ed.). New York, NY: Oxford University Press.

Burger, J. M. (2007). *Personality* (7th ed.). Belmont, TN: Thomson Higher Education.

Business Day. (2013). *Chamber of mines warns on electricity increases.* Retrieved September 5, 2014, from http://www.bdlive.co.za/national/labour/2013/02/01/chamber-of-mines-warns-on-electricity-increases.

Caplan, R. D., Cobb, S., French, J. R. P., Jr., van Harrison, R., & Pinneau, S. R., Jr. (1975). *Job demands and worker health.* Washington, DC: National Institute of Occupational Safety and Health.

Carr, J., Kelley, B., Keaton, R., & Albrecht, C. (2011). Getting to grips with stress in the workplace: Strategies for promoting a healthier, more productive environment. *Human Resource Management International Digest, 19*(4), 32–38.

Carrim, N. M. H. (2012). *The relationship amongst locus of control, self-determination and job satisfaction in call centres.* Unpublished master's thesis. University of Pretoria, Pretoria, South Africa.

Carrim, N. M. H. (2019). The in-betweeners: Racioethnic and masculine identity work of Indian male managers in the South African private sector. *The Journal of Men's Studies, 27*(1), 3–23.

Carrim, N. M. H., & Dresselhaus, F. (2019). Vicarious education, dialogue education and self-efficacy among Indian female students in a diversity management course. *Africa Education Review, 16*(5), 29–46.

Carrim, N. M. H., & Senne, Y. (2016). Challenges faced by South African human resource practitioners in multinational companies. In N. Zakaria, I. Abdul-Talib, & N. Osman (Eds.), *Handbook of research on impacts of international business and political affairs on the global economy* (pp. 133–153). Philadelphia, PA, USA: IGI Global Publishers.

Carrim, N. M. H., & Senne, Y. (2019). Life context model, intersectionality, and black feminist epistemology: Women managers in Africa. In E. T. Pereira & P. Paoloni (Eds.), *Handbook of research on women in management and the global labor market* (pp. 136–155). Philadelphia, PA, USA: IGI Global Publishers.

Cascio, W. F. (1991). *Applied psychology in personnel management* (4th ed.). Englewood Cliffs, NJ: Prentice Hall.

Catellano, C., & Plionis, E. (2006). Comparative analysis of three crisis intervention models applied to law enforcement first responders during 9/11 and hurricane Katrina. *Brief Treatment and Crisis Intervention, 6*(4), 326.

Caton, J. S., & Nowicki, S. (1997). Antecedents of individual differences in locus of control of reinforcement: A critical review. *Genetic, Social and General Psychology Monographs, 120,* 31–81.

Chen, J., & Silversthorne, C. (2008). The impact of locus of control on job stress, job performance and job satisfaction in Taiwan. *Leadership and Organisation Development Journal, 29*(7), 572–582.

Chen, J., & Wang, L. (2007). Locus of control and the three components of commitment to change. *Personality and Individual Differences, 42,* 503–512.

Choo, F. (1986). Job stress, job performance, and auditor personality characteristics. *Auditing: A Journal of Practice and Theory, 5*(2), 17–34.

Cole, A. H. (2010). Analysis of occupational stress and employees' health conditions in manufacturing companies. *Journal of Medical Sciences, 8*(2), 78–88.

Colligan, T. W., & Higgins, E. M. (2005). Workplace stress: Etiology and consequences. *Journal of Workplace Health, 21*(2), 90–97.

Cooper, C. L. (Ed.). (1998). *Theories of organizational stress.* Oxford: New York, NY.

Cooper, C. L., & Cartwright, S. (1994). Healthy mind, healthy organisation: A proactive approach to occupational stress. *Human Relations, 47,* 455–470.

Cooper, C. L., & Payne, R. (1978). *Stress at work.* Chichester: Wiley.

Correa, A. P., & Ferreira, M. C. (2011). The impact of environmental stressors and types of work contract on occupational stress. *The Spanish Journal of Psychology, 14*(1), 251–262.

Cox, T. (1978). *Stress.* London, UK: Macmillan.

Craighead, W. E., & Nemeroff, C. B. (2001). *The Corsini encyclopaedia of psychology and behavioural science* (3rd ed.). Hoboken, NJ: Wiley.

Creswell, J. W. (2008). *Research design: Qualitative, quantitative, and mixed methods approaches.* London: Sage.

Creswell, J. W. (2009). *Research design: Qualitative, quantitative, and mixed methods approaches* (3rd ed.). Thousand Oaks, CA: Sage.

Creswell, J. W., & Plano Clark, V. L. (2010). *Designing and conducting mixed methods research* (2nd ed.). Thousand Oaks, CA: Sage.

Critchley, H. D., Rotshtein, P., Nagai, Y., O'Doherty, J., Mathias, C. J., & Dolan, R. J. (2005). Activity in the human brain predicting differential heart rate responses to emotional facial expressions. *Neuroimage, 24*(3), 751–762.
Cüceloğlu, D. (1996). *İnsan ve davranışı*. İstanbul, Turkey: Remzi Kitabevi.
Cvetanovski, J., & Jex, S. M. (1994). Locus of control of unemployed people and its relationship to psychological and physical well-being. *Work & Stress, 8*, 60–67.
Daly, J., Kellehear, A., & Gliksman, M. (1997). *The public health researcher: A methodological approach*. Melbourne, Australia: Oxford University Press.
Dash, K. K. (2005). *Online research methods resource: Module—Selection of the research paradigm and methodology*. Retrieved August, 23, 2016, from Manchester Metropolitan University Website. http://www.celt.mmu.ac.uk/researchmethods/Modules/Selection_of_methodology/index.ph.
Davies, V. P. (2012). Fundamentals of occupational health hazard in organizations: An empirical studies. *International Journal of Educational Psychology and developmental Studies, 5*(2), 23–34.
De Simone, S., Cicotto, G., & Lampis, J. (2016). Occupational stress, job satisfaction and physical health in teachers. *Revue Européenne de Psychologie Appliquée, 66*, 65–77.
Department of Mineral Resources. (2010). *Amendment of the broad-based socio-economic empowerment charter for the South African mining and minerals industry*. Pretoria: Government Printer.
Desmond, P. A., & Hancock, P. A. (2001). Active and passive fatigue states. In P. A. Hancock & P. A. Desmond (Eds.), *Stress, workload, and fatigue*. Mahwah, NJ: Erlbaum.
Dhir, S. (2019). *The changing nature of work, leadership, and organizational culture in future ready organizations*. Published senior thesis. Retrieved from https://scholarship.claremont.edu/cgi/viewcontent.cgi?article=3092&context=cmc_theses.
Du Plessis, A. J., & Huntley, K. (2009). Challenges in a globalised context for international human resource managers in South African organisations. *International Review of Business Research Papers, 5*(1), 413–427.
Erez, A., & Judge, T. A. (2001). Relationship of core self-evaluations to goal setting, motivation, and performance. *Journal of Applied Psychology, 86*, 1270–1279.
Facts About South African Mining. (2012). Retrieved July 2, 2014, from http://www.anglogold.co.za/NR/rdonlyres/465A8D32-9DC8-4BFD-BE16-9F7B76F3F4F3/0/FactsaboutSouthAfricanmining.pdf.
Faucett, J. M., Corwyn, R. F., & Poling, T. H. (2012). Clergy role stress: Interactive effects of role ambiguity and role conflict on intrinsic job satisfaction. *Pastoral Psychology, 62*(3), 291–304.
Felizer, M. Y. (2010). Doing mixed methods research pragmatically: Implications for the rediscovery of pragmatism as a research paradigm. *Journal of Mixed Methods Research, 4*(1), 6–16.
Felton, S. M., & Cole, K. (2008). *Strategic management and workplace stress*. New York, NY: Macmillan Press.
Fereday, J., & Muir-Cochrane, E. (2006). Demonstrating rigor using thematic analysis: A hybrid approach of inductive and deductive coding and theme development. *International Journal of Qualitative Methods, 5*(1), Article 7. Retrieved August 15, 2016, from http://www.ualberta.ca/~iiqm/backissues/5_1/html/fereday.htm.
Field, A. P. (2005). *Discovering statistics using SPSS*. London, UK: Sage.
Financial Mail. (2013). *Unions unite against Eskom*. Retrieved August 8, 2014, from http://bundupower.co.za/news/unions-unite-against-eskom-financial-mail/.
Findley, M. J., & Cooper, H. M. (1983). Locus of control and academic achievement: A literature review. *Journal of Personality and Social Psychology, 4*(2), 419–427.
Fogarty, G. J., & Machin, M. A. (2003). *Discrepancy between preferred and actual levels of exposure to occupational stressors and resulting feelings of strain*. Queensland, Australia: University of Southern Queensland.
Fotinatos-Ventouratos, R., & Cooper, C. (2005). The role of gender and social class in work stress. *Journal of Managerial Psychology, 20*(1), 14–23.
Fox, S., & Spector, P. E. (1999). A model of work frustration—Aggression. *Journal of Organizational Behavior, 20*, 915–931.

French, J. R. P., Jr., Caplan, R. D., & Harrison, R. V. (1982). *The mechanisms of job stress and strain.* London, UK: Wiley.
Furnham, A., & Drakeley, R. J. (1993). Work locus of control and perceived organizational climate. *European Work and Organizational Psychologist, 3,* 1–9.
Furnham, A., & Steele, H. (1993). Measuring locus of control: A critique of general, children's, health- and work-related locus of control questionnaires. *British Journal of Psychology, 84,* 443–479.
Ganster, D. C., & Fusilier, M. R. (1989). Control in the workplace. In C. L. Cooper & I. T. Robertson (Eds.), *International review of industrial and organizational psychology* (pp. 235–280). Chichester, UK: Wiley.
Ganster, D. C., & Rosen, C. C. (2013). Work stress and employee health: A multidisciplinary review. *Journal of Management, 39*(5), 1085–1122.
Ganster, D. C., & Schaubroeck, J. (1991). Work stress and employee health. *Journal of Management, 17*(2), 235–271.
Gastrow, P. (2001). *Theft from South African mines and refineries: The illicit market for gold and platinum.* Retrieved August 25, 2014, from http://www.iss.co.za/Pubs/Monographs/No54/Chap1.html.
Gatchel, R. J., & Kishino, N. (2011). Pain, musculoskeletal injuries and return to work. In J. C. Quick & L. E. Tetrick (Eds.), *Handbook of occupational health psychology* (pp. 265–276). Washington, DC, USA: American Psychological Association.
Gavin, J. F., & Axelford, W. L. (1977). Managerial stress and strain in a mining organization. *Journal of Occupational Behaviour, 11,* 66–74.
Gilroy, B. M., Gries, T., & Naudé, W. A. (2006). *Multinational enterprises, foreign direct investment and growth in Africa: South African perspectives.* Dordrecht, Netherlands: Springer Science & Business Media.
Gist, M. E., & Mitchell, T. R. (1992). Self-efficacy: A theoretical analysis of its determinants and malleability. *Academy of Management Review, 12*(2), 183–211.
Graffeo, L. C., & Silvestri, L. (2006). Relationship between locus of control and health-related variables. *Education, 126*(3), 593–596.
Graham, J. W. (1991). An essay on organizational citizenship behavior. *Employee Responsibilities and Rights Journal, 4,* 249–270.
Greenhaus, J. H., & Beutell, N. J. (1985). Sources of conflict between work and family roles. *Academy of Management Review, 10,* 76–88.
Greenhaus, J. H., Callanan, G. A., & Godshalh, V. M. (2000). *Career management* (3rd ed.). London, UK: Thomson.
Guba, E. G., & Lincoln, Y. S. (1989). *Fourth generation evaluation.* Newbury Park, CA: Sage.
Gutek, B., Searle, S., & Klepa, L. (1991). Rational versus gender role expectations for work-family conflict. *Journal of Applied Psychology, 76,* 560–568.
Hackman, J. R., & Oldham, G. R. (1980). *Work redesign.* Reading, MA: Addison-Wesley.
Haine, R. A., Ayers, T. S., Sandler, I. A., Wolchick, S. A., & Weyer, J. L. (2003). Locus of control and self-esteem as stress-moderators or stress-mediators in parentally bereaved children. *Death Studies, 27*(7), 619–641.
Hakim, A. L., & Sutrisno, S. (2018). The effect of work stress on turnover intention with work satisfaction and commitment as intervening variable (Study at PT. Infomedia Solusi Humanika, Malang). *European Journal of Business and Management, 10*(12), 85–95.
Hamid, P. N. (1994). Self-monitoring, locus of control, and social encounters of Chinese and New Zealand students. *Journal of Cross-cultural Psychology, 25,* 353–368.
Hammer, L. B., Kossek, E. E., Anger, W. K., Bodner, T., & Zimmerman, K. L. (2011). Clarifying work–family intervention processes: The roles of work–family conflict and family-supportive supervisor behaviors. *Journal of Applied Psychology, 96*(1), 134–145.
Hancock, P. A., & Desmond, P. A. (2001). *Stress, workload and fatigue.* Mahwah, NJ: Lawrence Erlbaum.

Haque, A. U., & Aston, J. (2016). A relationship between occupational stress and organisational commitment of IT sector's employees in contrasting economies. *Polish Journal of Management Studies, 14*(1), 95–105.

Harrits, G. S. (2011). More than method? A discussion of paradigm differences within mixed methods research. *Journal of Mixed Methods Research, 5,* 150–166.

Hart, P. M. (1994). Teacher quality of work life: Integrating work experiences, psychological distress and morale. *Journal of Occupational and Organizational Psychology, 67,* 109–132.

Headey, B., & Wearing, A. J. (1992). *Understanding happiness: A theory of subjective well-being.* Melbourne, Australia: Longman Cheshire.

Hellriegel, D., Jackson, S. E., & Slocum, J. W. (1999). *Management.* Cincinnati, OH: South-Western.

Hendel, D. D., & Horn, A. S. (2008). The relationship between academic life conditions and perceived sources of faculty stress over time. *Journal of Human Behavior in the Social Environment, 17*(1–2), 61–88.

Hewitt, P. L., & Flett, G. (1996). Personality traits and the coping process. In M. Zeidner & N. S. Endler (Eds.), *Handbook of coping: Theory, research, applications* (pp. 410–433). New York, NY: Wiley.

Hill, E. J., Jacob, J. I., Shannon, L. L., Brennan, R. T., Blanchard, V. L., & Martinengo, G. (2008). Exploring the relationship of workplace flexibility, gender, and lide stage to family-to-work conflict, and stress and burnout. *Community, Work and Family, 11*(2), 165–181.

Holmlund-Rytkönen, M., & Strandvik, T. (2005). Stress in business relationships. *Journal of Business & Industrial Marketing, 20*(1), 12–22.

Hopkins, M. M., & Yonker, R. D. (2015). Managing conflict with emotional intelligence: Abilities that make a difference. *Journal of Management Development.*

Horwitz, F. M. (2012). Evolving human resource management in Southern African multinational firms: Towards an Afro-Asian nexus. *The International Journal of Human Resource Management, 23*(14), 2938–2958.

Horwitz, F. M., Browning, V., Jain, H., & Steenkamp, A. J. (2002). Human resource practices and discrimination in South Africa: Overcoming the apartheid legacy. *International Journal of Human Resource Management, 13*(7), 1105–1118.

Hoyle, R. H., Harris, M. J., & Judd, C. M. (2002). *Research methods in social relations.* New York, NY: Wadsworth.

Hui, C. H. (1982). Locus of control: A review of cross-cultural research. *International Journal of Intercultural Relations, 6,* 301–323.

Iorvaa, T. (2004). *Introduction to health education.* Nigeria, Makurdi: Adeka Publishers Company Nigeria Ltd.

Irawanto, D. W., Noermiyati, & Primasari, D. (2015). The effect of occupational stress on work performance of female employees: Study in Indonesia. *Asia-Pacific Journal of Management Research and Innovation, 11*(4), 336–345.

Ivancevich, J. M., Konopasle, R., & DeFrank, R. S. (2003). Business travel stress: A model, propositions and managerial implications. *Work and Stress, 17*(2), 138–157.

Ivancevich, J. M., & Matteson, M. T. (1999). *Organizational behaviour and management* (5th ed.). Singapore: Irwin McGraw-Hill.

Ivankova, N., Creswell, J., & Plano Clark, V. (2012). Foundations and approaches to mixed methods research. In K. Maree (Ed.), *First steps in research.* Van Schaik: Pretoria, South Africa.

Jahanzeb, H. (2010). The impact of job stress on job satisfaction among academic Faculty of a mega distance learning institution in Pakistan: A case study of Allama Iqbal Open University. *Mustang Journal of Business & Ethics, 1,* 31–48.

Jain, K. K., Jabeen, F., Mishra, V., & Gupta, N. (2007). Job satisfaction as related to organizational climate and occupational stress: A case study of Indian Oil. *International Review of Business Research Papers, 3*(5), 193–208.

Jayashree, R. (2010). Stress management with special reference to public sector bank employees in Chennai. *International Journal of Enterprise and Innovation Management Studies, 1*(3), 34–35.

Jeffrey, K., Mahoney, S., Michaelson, J., & Abdullah, S. (2014). *Well-being at work: A review of the literature*. New Economics Foundation. Retrieved June 5, 2016, from http://www.neweconomics.org/issues/entry/well-being.

Judge, T. A., & Bono, J. E. (2001). Relationship of core self-evaluation traits, self-esteem, generalized self-efficacy, locus of control, and emotional stability—With job satisfaction and job performance: A meta-analysis. *Journal of Applied Psychology, 86*(1), 80–92.

Kalbers, L. P., & Fogarty, T. J. (2005). Antecedents to internal auditor burnout. *Journal of Managerial Issues, 1,* 101–118.

Kalechstein, A. D., & Nowicki, S. (1997). A meta-analytic examination of the relationship between control expectancies and academic achievement: An 11-year follow-up to Findley and Cooper. *Genetic, Social and General Psychology Monographs, 123*(1), 27–56.

Kandula, S. R. (2003). *Human resource management in practice: With 300 models, techniques and tools*. New Delhi, India: Prentice-Hall.

Kaplan, S., & Tetrick, L. E. (2011). Workplace safety and accidents: An industrial and organizational psychology perspective. In S. Zedeck (Ed.), *Handbook of industrial and organizational psychology* (pp. 455–472). Washington, DC, USA: American Psychological Association.

Karasek, R. A. (1979). Job demands, job decision latitude, and mental strain: Implications for job redesign. *Administrative Science Quarterly, 24,* 285–308.

Karasek Jr., R. A. (1979). Job demands, job decision latitude, and mental strain: Implications for job redesign. *Administrative Science Quarterly, 25,* 285–308.

Karasek, R., & Theorell, T. (1990). *Healthy work: Stress, productivity and the reconstruction of working life*. New York, NY: Basic Books.

Kashima, Y., Foddy, M., & Platow, M. J. (2002). *Self and identity: Personal, social, and symbolic*. Mahwah, NJ: Lawrence Erlbaum.

Kearney, L. (2012). *Mining and minerals in South Africa*. South Africa.info. Retrieved February 23, 2014, from www.southafrica.info/business/economy/sectors/mining.htm#.Uwr3N4aQZnA.

Keenan, A., & McBain, G. D. M. (1979). Effects of type A behavior, intolerance of ambiguity, and locus of control on the relationship between role stress and work-related outcomes. *Journal of Occupational Psychology, 52*(4), 277–285.

Kirchner, M. J. (2003). *The relationship between locus of control and academic achievement among risk students*. Unpublished master's dissertation. University or Pretoria, Pretoria, South Africa.

Kivilu, J. M., & Rogers, W. T. (1997). A multi-level analysis of cultural experience and gender influences on causal attributions to perceived performance in mathematics. *International Development Research Centre (IDRC),* 25–37.

König, C. J., Debus, M. E., Häusler, S., Lendenmann, N., & Kleinmann, M. (2010). Examining occupational self-efficacy, work locus of control and communication as moderators of the job insecurity—Job performance relationship. *Economic and Industrial Democracy, 31*(2), 231–247.

Kossek, E. E., Kalliath, E. E., & Kalliath, P. (2012). Achieving employee wellbeing in a changing work environment: An expert commentary on current scholarship. *International Journal of Manpower, 33*(7), 738–753.

Kyriacou, C. (2001). Teacher stress: Directions for future research. *Educational Review, 53*(1), 27–35.

Kyriacou, C., & Sutcliffe, J. (1978). A model of teacher stress. *Education Studies, 4,* 1–6.

Lacey, A., & Luff, D. (2007). *Qualitative data analysis*. National Institute for Health Research: Sheffield Trent RDSU.

LaDou, J. (2007). *Current occupational and environmental medicine* (4th ed.). New York, NY: McGraw-Hill.

Lamontagne, A. D., Keegel, T., Louie, A. M., Ostry, A., & Landsbergis, P. A. (2007). A systematic review of the job-stress intervention evaluation literature 1990–2005. *International Journal of Occupational and Environmental Health, 13,* 268–80.

Landsbergis, P. A., Schnall, P. L., Belkic, K. L., Baker, D., Schwartz, J. E., & Pickering, T. G. (2011). Workplace and cardiovascular disease: Relevance and potential role for occupational health psychology. In J. C. Quick & L. E. Tetrick (Eds.), *Handbook of occupational health psychology* (pp. 37–54). Washington, DC, USA: American Psychological Association.

Landy, F. J., & Conte, J. M. (2007). *Work in the 21st century: An introduction to industrial and organisational psychology* (2nd ed.). Danvers, MA: Blackwell.

Lasalvia, A., & Tansella, M. (2011). Occupational stress and job burnout in mental health. *Epidemiology and Psychiatric Sciences, 20*(4), 279–285.

Lawler, E., & Hall, D. (1970). Relationship of Job characteristics to job involvement, satisfaction, and intrinsic motivation. *Journal of Applied Psychology, 54,* 305–312.

Lazarus, R. S., & Folkman, S. (1984). *Stress, appraisal, and coping.* New York, NY: Springer.

Leedy, P. D., & Ormrod, J. E. (2005). *Practical research: Planning and design* (8th ed.). Upper Saddle River, NJ: Pearson.

Lefcourt, H. M. (1976). *The locus of control: Current trends in theory and research.* New York, NY: Wiley.

Lefcourt, H. M. (1992). Durability and impact of the locus of control construct. *Psychological Bulletin, 112,* 411–414.

Leon, P. (2013). *Challenges to the South African mining industry in the wake of Marikana and Mangaung.* Retrieved September 7, 2014, from http://www.capetownpc.org.za/docs/speeches/Challenges-facing-the-South-African-mining-industry-Comments-by-Peter-Leon-to-the-Cape-Town-Press.pdf.

Levenson, H. (1973). Multidimensational locus of control in psychiatric patients. *Journal of Consulting and Clinical Psychology, 41,* 397–404.

Liu, C., Spector, P. E., & Shi, L. (2007). Cross-national job stress: A quantitative and qualitative study. *Journal of Organizational Behavior, 28,* 209–239.

Lopopolo, R. B. (2002). The relationship of role-related variables to job satisfaction and commitment to the organization in a restructured hospital environment. *Physical Therapy, 82*(10), 984–999.

Lu, L., Wu, H., & Cooper, C. L. (1999). Perceived work stress and locus of control: A combined quantitative and qualitative approach. *Research and Practice in Human Resource Management, 7*(1), 1–15.

Lundberg, U. (2002). Psychophysiology of work: Stress, gender, endocrine response, and work-related upper extremity disorders. *American Journal of Industrial Medicine, 41*(5), 383–392.

Lutzen, K., Cronqvist, A., Magnusson, A., & Andersson, L. (2003). Moral stress: Synthesis of a concept. *Nursing Ethics, 10*(3), 312–322.

Macan, T. H., Trusty, M. L., & Trimble, S. K. (1996). Spector's work locus of control scale: Dimensionality and validity evidence. *Educational and Psychological Measurement, 56*(2), 349–357.

Malik, A., Björkqvist, K., & Österman, K. (2017). Factors associated with occupational stress among University Teachers in Pakistan and Finland. *Journal of Educational, Health and Community Psychology, 6*(2), 1–14.

Malik, N., & Dhar, R. L. (2017). Authentic leadership and its impact on extra role behaviour of nurses. *Personnel Review, 46*(2), 277–296.

Manshor, A. T., Fontaine, R., & Choy, C. S. (2003). Occupational stress among managers: A Malaysian survey. *Journal of Managerial Psychology, 18*(6), 622–628.

Maram, A., & Miller, K. (1998). An empirical assessment of the construct work locus of control. *Journal of Industrial Psychology, 24*(3), 48–51.

Markow, D., & Pieters, A. (2012). *Metlife survey of the American teacher: Teachers, parents, and the economy.* Retrieved August 29, 2014, from www.metlife.com.

Martiz, T. (2002). A comparison between the June 1991 and Series 2000 JBCC preliminaries editions. *Acta Structilia, 9*(1), 79–93.

Maslach, C. (2006). Understanding job burnout. In A. M. Rossi, P. L. Perrewe, and S. L. Sauter (Eds.), *Stress and quality of working life: Current perspectives in occupational health* (pp. 37–51). Greenwich, CT, USA: Information Age Publishing.

Meyer, R. M., Li, A., Klaristenfeld, J., & Gold, J. I. (2015). Pediatric novice nurses: Examining compassion fatigue as a mediator between stress exposure and compassion satisfaction, burnout, and job satisfaction. *Journal of pediatric nursing, 30*(1), 174–183.

Millward, L. J. (2005). *Understanding occupational & organizational psychology*. London, UK: Sage.

Mohammad Mosadeghrad, A. (2014). Occupational stress and its consequences: Implications for health policy and management. *Leadership in Health Services, 27*(3), 224–239.

Mohapatra, M., & Gupta, A. (2010). Relationship of emotional intelligence with work values & internal locus of control: A study of managers in a public sector organization. *Vilakshan: The XIMB Journal of Management, 7*(2), 1–20.

Monat, A., & Lazarus, R. S. (1991). *Stress and coping: An anthology*. New York, NY: Columbia University Press.

Morgan, B. (1997). *Images of organization* (2nd ed.). Thousand Oaks, CA: Sage.

Moronkola, O. A. (2003). *Essays on issues of mental health*. Ibadan: Royal People (NIG) Ltd.

Mosadeghrad, A. M. (2013). Occupational stress and turnover intention: Implications for nursing management. *International Journal of Health Policy and Management, 1*(2), 169–179.

Mostert, F. F., Rothmann, S., Mostert, K., & Nell, K. (2008). Outcomes of occupational stress in a higher education institution. *Southern African Business Review, 12*(3), 102–127.

Mouton, J. (2001). *How to succeed in your master's and doctoral studies: A South African guide and resource book*. Pretoria, South Africa: Van Schaik.

Moyle, P. (1995). The role of negative affectivity in the stress process: Tests of alternative methods. *Journal of Organizational Behaviour, 16*, 647–668.

Muhonen, T., & Torkelson, E. (2004). Work locus of control and its relationship to health and job satisfaction from a gender perspective. *Stress and Health, 20*, 21–28.

Murphy, J. (2002). *What can business do?* (pp. 4–7). August/September: A Succeed Magazine Special Publication.

Narahari, C. L., & Koneru, D. K. (2017). A study on the role of occupational stress in organisations. *International Journal of Engineering Techonology, Engineering, Management & Applied Science, 5*, 53–59.

Nelson, D. L., & Burke, R. J. (2000). Women executives: Health, stress, and success. *Academy of Management Perspectives, 14*(2), 107–121.

Nelson, D. L., & Burke, R. J. (2002). *Gender, work stress and health*. Washington, DC: American Psychological Association.

Nelson, D. L., & Simmons, B. L. (2011) Savoring eustress while coping with distress: The holistic model of stress. In J. C. Quick & L. E. Tetrick (Eds.), *Handbook of occupational health psychology* (2nd ed., pp. 55–74). Washington, DC, USA: American Psychological Association.

Neuman, W. L. (2011). *Social research methods: Qualitative and quantitative approaches* (7th ed.). Boston, MA: Pearson/Allyn & Bacon.

O'Brien, G. E. (1983). Locus of control, work, and retirement. In H. M. Lefcourt (Ed.), *Research in locus of control* (Vol. 3). New York, NY: Academic Press.

Oosthuizen, M. M. (2016). *The relationship between occupational stress and work locus of control amongst South African management: An exploratory study*. Unpublished M.Com. dissertation. University of Pretoria, Pretoria, South Africa.

Organ, D. W. (1997). Toward an explication of 'morale' in search of the M factor. In C. L. Cooper & S. E. Jackson (Eds.), *Creating tomorrow's organizations: A handbook for future research in organizational behavior* (pp. 493–504). Chichester, UK: John Wiley.

Organizing Your Social Sciences Research Paper. (2014). Retrieved July 1, 2014, from http://libguides.usc.edu/writingguide.

Orpen, C. (1992). The work locus of control scale as a predictor of employee attitudes and behaviour: A validity study. *Journal of Human Behavior, 2*, 35–37.

O'Toole, J. (Ed.). (1974). *Work and the quality of life*. Cambridge, MA: MIT Press.

Park, Y. S., & Kim, U. (1998). Locus of control, attributional style, and academic achievement: Comparative analysis of Korean, Korean-Chinese, and Chinese students. *Asian Journal of Social Psychology, 1*(2), 191–208.

Patton, M. Q. (2002). *Qualitative research and evaluation methods*. Thousand Oaks, CA: Sage.

Pearlstein, T. B., Zlotnick, C., Battle, C. L., Stuart, S., O'Hara, M. W., Price, A. B., et al. (2006). Patient choice of treatment for postpartum depression: A pilot study. *Archives of Women's Mental Health, 9*(6), 303–308.

Peterson, C., & Seligman, M. E. (1984). Causal explanations as a risk factor for depression: Theory and evidence. *Psychological Review, 91*(3), 347–374.

Phares, E. J. (1976). *Locus of control in personality*. Morristown, NJ: General Learning Press.

Pisanti, R., van der Doef, M., Maes, S., Lazzari, D., & Bertini, M. (2011). Job characteristics, organizational conditions, and distress/well-being among Italian and Dutch nurses: A cross-national comparison. *International Journal of Nursing Studies, 48*(7), 829–837.

Pramode, D. (2019). Effect of occupational stress on turnover intention: A study with special attention to information technology employees in Chennai. *Journal of the Gujarat Research Society, 21*(15s2), 111–118.

Price Waterhouse Coopers. (2012). *SA Mine: Highlighting trends in the South African mining industry*. Retrieved September 10, 2014, from http://www.pwc.co.za/en/publications/sa-mine.jhtml.

Privitera, M. R., Rosenstein, A. H., Plessow, F., & LoCastro, T. M. (2015). Physician burnout and occupational stress: An inconvenient truth with unintended consequences. *Journal of Hospital Administration, 4*(1), 27–35.

Quelch, J. A., & Austin, J. E. (2012). Should multinationals invest in Africa? *Image,* 1–8.

Quick, J. C., & Henderson, D. F. (2016). Occupational stress: Preventing suffering, enhancing wellbeing. *International Journal of Environmental Research and Public Health, 13*(5), 459–465.

Quick, J. C., Joplin, J. R., Nelson, D. L., Mangelsdorff, A. D., & Fiedler, E. (1996). Self-reliance and military service training outcomes. *Military Psychology, 8*(4), 279–293.

Quick, J. C., Quick, J. D., Nelson, D. L., & Hurrell, J. J. (1997). *Preventive Stress Management in Organizations*. Washington, DC: American Psychological Association.

Rahim, A. (1996). Stress, strain, and their moderators: An empirical comparison of entrepreneurs and managers. *Journal of Small Business Management, 34,* 46–58.

Rahim, S. A. (1994). Participatory development communication as a dialogical process. In S. A. White, K. S. Nair, & J. Ascroft (Eds.), *Participatory communication: Working for change and development*. New Delhi, India: Sage.

Rechel, B., Buchan, J., & McKee, M. (2009). The impact of health facilities on healthcare workers' well-being and performance. *International Journal of Nursing Studies, 46*(7), 1025–1034.

Rice, P. L., & Ezzy, D. (1999). *Qualitative research methods: A health focus*. South Melbourne, Australia: Oxford University Press.

Ridner, S. H. (2004). Psychological distress: Concept analysis. *Journal of Advanced Nursing, 45*(5), 536–545.

Rigotti, T., Schyns, B., & Mohr, G. (2008). A short version of the occupational self-efficacy scale: Structural and construct validity across five countries. *Journal of Career Assessment, 16,* 238–255.

Roberts, J. A., Lapidus, R. S., & Chonko, L. B. (1997). Sales people and stress: The moderating role of locus of control on work stressors and felt stress. *Journal of Marketing Theory and Practice, 5,* 93–108.

Robinson, L. D. (2017a). *The work-family interface and burnout in sole and partnered working Australian mothers*. Unpublished Ph.D. thesis. University of Wollongong, Wollongong.

Robinson, L. D. (2017b). *The work-family interface and burnout in sole and partnered working Australian mothers*. Published doctoral thesis. University of Wollongong, Australia. Retrieved from https://ro.uow.edu.au/theses1/69.

Rodríguez, I., Bravo, M. J., Peiró, J. M., & Schaufeli, W. (2001). The demands-control-support model, locus of control and job dissatisfaction: A longitudinal study. *Work & Stress, 15*(2), 97–114.

Rothmann, S., & Joubert, J. H. M. (2007). Job demands, job resources, burnout and work engagement of managers at a platinum mine in the North West Province. *South African Journal of Business Management, 38*(3), 49–61.

Rotter, J. B. (1966). Generalised expectancies for internal versus external control of reinforcement. *Psychological Monographs, 80*(1), 169–214.

Rotter, J. B. (1975). Some problems and misconceptions related to the construct of internal versus external control of reinforcement. *Journal of Clinical and Consulting Psychology, 43,* 56–67.

Sadri, G., Marcoulides, G. A., Cooper, C. L., & Kirkcaldy, B. (1996). Testing a model of occupational stress across different countries. *Journal of Business and Management, 20,* 10–29.

Saunders, M., Lewis, P., & Thornhill, A. (2007). *Research methods for business students* (4th ed.). Essex, UK: Pearson Education.

Saunders, M., Lewis, P., & Thornhill, A. (2009). *Research methods for business students* (5th ed.). London, UK: Pearson Education.

Sauter, S. L., & Murphy, L. R. (1995). *Organizational risk factors for job stress.* Washington, DC: American Psychological Association.

Schreuder, A. M. G., & Coetzee, M. (2008). *Careers: An organisational perspective.* Cape Town, South Africa: Juta.

Schuler, R. S. (1980, April). Definition and conceptualization of stress in organizations. In *Organizational behavior and human performance* (p.189). Adapted from Robbins (2005).

Schultz, J. M. (2009). *Why parents choose a catholic school: A social understanding.* Unpublished doctoral thesis. Duquesne University of Pittsburgh, Pittsburgh, United States of America.

Scott, S. L., Carper, T. M., Middleton, M., White, R., & Renk, K. (2010). Relationship among locus of control, coping behaviours, and level of worry following exposure to hurricanes. *Journal of Loss and Trauma, 15*(2), 123–137.

Seel, K., & Angelini, A. (2004). Strengthening the capacity of executive directors. Paper presented at the Association for Research on Nonprofit and Voluntary Action, Los Angeles, November 2004.

Sekiguchi, T. (2004). Person-organisation fit and person-job fit in employee selection: A review of the literature. *Osaka Keidai Ronshu, 54*(6), 179–196.

Selye, H. (1976). *Stress in health and disease.* Reading, MA: Butterworth.

Semmer, N. K. (2000). Control at work: Issues of specificity, generality, and legitimacy. In P. J. Walter & A. Grob (Eds.), *Control of human behavior, mental processes, and consciousness: Essays in honor of the 60th birthday of August Flammer* (pp. 555–564). Mahwah, NJ: Lawrence Erlbaum Associates.

Shabazz, K. M. (2007). *The effects of environment and age on locus of control, self-efficacy, and self-esteem of military and non-military students' academic achievement.* Unpublished doctoral thesis. Touro University International, Cypress, California, United States of America.

Siegrist, J. (1996). Adverse health effects of high-effort/low-reward conditions. *Journal of Occupational Health Psychology, 1*(1), 27–41.

Siu, O., Spector, C. L., Lu, L., & Yu, S. (2002). Managerial stress in Greater China: The direct and moderator effects of coping strategies and Work locus of control. *Applied Psychology: An International Review, 53*(4), 608–632.

Smith, C., & Short, P. M. (2001). Integrating technology to improve the efficiency of qualitative data analysis—A note on methods. *Qualitative Sociology, 24*(3), 401–407. https://doi.org/10.1023/A:1010643025038.

Smith, L. O. (2011). Workplace stress and organizational intervention programmes: An holistic approach. *Journal of Information Technology and Management, 2*(2), 45–56.

Smith, P. B., Trompenaars, F., & Dugan, S. (1995). The Rotter locus of control scale in 43 countries: A test of cultural relativity. *International Journal of Psychology, 30,* 377–400.

Smith, V. L. (2003). *Analysis of locus of control and educational level utilizing the internal control index.* Unpublished master's dissertation. The Graduate College of Marshall University, Marshall University, Huntington, England.

South African History Online. (2014). *Timeline of the Marikana Massacre 2012–2013*. Retrieved August 28, 2014, from http://www.sahistory.org.za/article/timelinemarikana-massacre-2012-2013.

Special Task Force to the Secretary of Health, Education and Welfare. (1973). *Work in America*. Cambridge, MA: MIT Press.

Spector, P. E. (1982). Behavior in organizations as a function of employee's locus of control. *Psychological Bulletin, 91,* 482–497.

Spector, P. E. (1986). Perceived control of employees: A meta-analysis of studies concerning autonomy and participation at work. *Human Relations, 39,* 1005–1016.

Spector, P. E. (1988). Development of the Work locus of control scale. *Journal of Occupational Psychology, 61,* 335–340.

Spector, P. E. (1992). *Summated rating scale construction*. Newbury Park, CA: Sage.

Spector, P. E. (1998). A control theory of the job stress process. In C. L. Cooper (Ed.), *Theories of organizational stress* (pp. 153–169). Oxford: New York, NY.

Spector, P. E. (2002). Employee control and occupational stress. *Current Directions in Psychosocial Science, 11*(4), 133–136.

Spector, P. E., & Jex, S. M. (1998). Development of four self-report measures of job stressors and strain: Interpersonal conflict at work scale, organizational constraints scale, quantitative workload inventory, and physical symptoms inventory. *Journal of Occupational Health Psychology, 3,* 356–367.

Spector, P., & O'Connell, B. J. (1994). The contribution of personality traits, negative, locus of control and Type A to the subsequent reports of job stressor and job strains. *Journal of Occupational and Organisational Psychology, 67*(1), 1–11.

Spector, P. E., Sanchez, J. I., Ling Sui, O., Salgado, J., & Ma, J. (2004). Eastern versus Western control beliefs at work: An investigation of secondary control, socioinstrumental control, and WLOC in China and the US. *Applied Psychology: An International Review, 53*(1), 38–60.

Spies, J. (2004). *The relationship between occupational stressors, occupational stress and burnout among trauma unit nursing staff*. Unpublished master's dissertation. University of Pretoria, Pretoria, South Africa.

Sprung, J. M., & Jex, S. M. (2012). Work locus of control as a moderator of the relationship between work stressors and counterproductive work behavior. *International Journal of Stress Management, 19*(4), 272–281.

Steyn, C., & Bell, D. (2015). *Management index report 2014/ 2015*. Retrieved June 5, 2016, from http://www.usb-ed.com/ManagementIndexReport/MIR2015.pdf.

Stipek, D. J., & Weisz, J. R. (1981). Perceived personal control and academic achievement. *Review of Education, 51,* 101–137.

Storm Pallesen, E. (2007). *Work-related stress and health and stress among hotel employees in Malmo*. Unpublished master's dissertation. Kristianstad University, Kristianstad, Sweden.

Strauss, A., & Corbin, J. (1998). *Basics of qualitative research: Techniques and procedures for developing grounded theory* (2nd ed.). Thousand Oaks, CA: Sage.

Stress. (n.d.). *In Merriam-Webster.com*. Retrieved from http://www.merriam-webster.com/dictionary/stress.

Strydom, H. (2011). Ethical aspects of research in the social sciences and human services professions. In A. S. De Vos, H. Strydom, C. B. Fouché, & C. S. L. Delport (Eds.), *Research at grass roots for the social sciences and human service professions* (4th ed.). Pretoria, South Africa: Van Schaik.

Taylor, S. E., Klein, L. C., Lewis, B. P., Gruenewald, T. L., Gurung, R. A., & Updegraff, J. A. (2000). Biobehavioral responses to stress in females: Tend-and-befriend, not fight-or-flight. *Psychological Review, 107*(3), 411–420.

Teddlie, C., & Tashakkori, A. (2009). *Foundations of mixed methods research: Integrating quantitative and qualitative approaches in the social and behavioral sciences*. Thousand Oaks, CA: Sage.

Thomas, J. C., & Hersen, M. (2002). *Handbook of mental health in the workplace*. Thousand Oaks, CA: Sage.

Thomas, L. S., & Valli, A. (2006). Levels of occupational stress in doctors working in a South African public-sector hospital: Issues in medicine: SAMJ forum. *South African Medical Journal, 96*(11), 1162–1168.

Tong, M., Arora, K., White, M. M., & Nichols, R. A. (2011). Role of key aromatic residues in the ligand-binding domain of α7 nicotinic receptors in the agonist action of β-amyloid. *Journal of Biological Chemistry, 286*(39), 34373–34381.

Tong, J., & Wang, L. (2006). Validation of locus of control scale in Chinese organizations. *Personality and Individual Differences, 41*, 941–950.

Topper, E. F. (2007). Stress in the library. *Journal of New Library, 108*(11/12), 561–564.

Trochim, W. M. K. (2006). *Qualitative measures*. Retrieved August 30, 2016, from http://www.socialresearchmethods.net/kb/qual.php.

Tsutsumi, A., & Kawakami, N. (2004). A review of empirical studies on the model of effort—Reward imbalance at work: Reducing occupational stress by implementing a new theory. *Social Science and Medicine, 59*, 2335–2359.

Turner, H. A., & Jackson, D. A. (2009). On the stability of wage differences and productivity-based wage policies: An international analysis. *British Journal of Industrial Relations, 7*(1), 1–18.

Uguak, U. A., Elias, H. B., Uli, J., & Suandi, T. (2001). The influence of causal elements of locus of control on academic achievement satisfaction. *Journal of Instructional Psychology, 34*(2), 121–128.

Van Niekerk, M. (2011). *The relationship between occupational stress and locus of control among nurses*. Unpublished master's dissertation. University of Pretoria, Pretoria, South Africa.

Van Rensburg, H., Basson, J., & Carrim, N. (2011). Human resource management as a profession in South Africa. *SA Journal of Human Resource Management/SA Tydskrif vir Menslikehulpbronbestuur, 9*(1).

Van Zyl, E. S., & Van der Walt, H. S. (1991). *Manual for the experience of work and life circumstances questionnaire (WLQ)*. Pretoria, South Africa: Human Sciences Research Council.

Varadnyan, V. (2011). *Panorama of psychology*. Central Milton Keynes: Author House.

Verma, V. K. (1998). Conflict management. In J. Pinto (Ed.), *The Project Management Institute project management handbook*. ISBN 0-7879-4013-5.

Wahyuni, D. (2012). The research design maze: Understanding paradigms, cases methods and methodologies. *Journal of Applied Management Accounting Research, 10*(1), 69–80.

Wallston, K. A. (1992). Hocus-pocus, the focus isn't strictly on locus: Rotter's social learning theory modified for health. *Cognitive Therapy and Research, 16*(2), 183–199.

Watson, D. (1988). Intra-individual and interindividual analyses of positive and negative affect: Their relation to health complaints, perceived stress, and daily activities. *Journal of Personality and Social Psychology, 54*, 1020–1030.

Webster, R. E. (2006). *CLEP: Introduction to educational psychology*. Piscataway, NY: Research and Education Association.

Weiner, B. (1972). *Theories of motivation: From mechanism to cognition*. Chicago, IL: Markham.

Weiner, B. (1979). A theory of motivation for some classroom experiences. *Journal of Education, 71*, 3–25.

Weiner, B. (1985). An attributional theory of achievement motivation and emotion. *Psychological Review, 92*, 548–573.

Weiner, B. (1995). *Judgments of responsibility: A foundation for a theory of social conduct*. New York, NY: Guilford Press.

Welman, C., Kruger, F., & Mitchell, B. (2012). *Research methodology* (3rd ed.). Cape Town, South Africa: Oxford University Press Southern Africa.

Weymer, R. A. (2002). Factors affecting students' performance in sixth grade modular technology education. *Journal of Technology Education, 13*, 33–46.

Whiteside, A., & Sunter, C. (2002). *AIDS—The challenge for South Africa*. Cape Town, South Africa: Human & Rousseau.

Wickham, M., & Woods, M. (2005). Reflecting on the strategic use of CAQDAS to manage and report on the qualitative research report. *The Qualitative Report, 10*(4), 687–702.

Wildemuth, B. M. (1993). Post-positivistic research: Two examples of methodological pluralism. *Library Quarterly, 63,* 450–468.

Wilski, M., Chmielewski, B., & Tomczak, M. (2015). Work locus of control and burnout in Polish physiotherapists: The mediating effect of coping styles. *International Journal of Occupational Medicine and Environmental Health, 28*(5), 875.

Wöcke, A., Bendixen, M., & Rijamampianina, R. (2007). Building flexibility into multi-national human resource strategy: A study of four South African multinational enterprises. *International Journal of Human Resource Management, 18*(5), 829–844.

Wolk, S., & Bloom, D. (1978). *The interactive effects of locus of control and situational stress upon performance accuracy and time.* Retrieved April 5, 2014, from http://interruptions.net/literature/Wolk-JP78.pdf.

Wood, M. J., & Kerr, J. C. (2011). *Basic steps in planning and nursing research: From question to proposal* (7th ed.). Sudbury, Canada: Jones & Bartlett.

Wrenn, B., Stevens, R. E., & Loudon, D. L. (2006). *Marketing research: Test and cases* (2nd ed.). Binghamton, NY: Best Business Books.

Yahaya, N., Yahaya, A., Tamyes, F. A., Ismail, J., & Jaalam, S. (2010). The effect of various modes of occupational stress, job satisfaction, intention to leave and absenteeism companies commission of Malaysia. *Australian Journal of Basic and Applied Sciences, 4*(7), 1676–1684.

Zahra, S. S., Khan, M. I., Imran, M., Aman, Q., & Ali, R. (2018). The relationship between job stress and turnover intentions in the pesticide sector of Pakistan: An employee behavior perspective. *Management Issues in Healthcare System, 4,* 1–12.

Zainudin, A., Junaidah, H. A., & Nazmi, M. Z. (2010). Modeling job satisfaction and work commitment among lecturers: A case of UITM Kelantan. *Journal of Statistical Modeling and Analytics, 1*(2), 45–59.

The manufacturer's authorised representative in the EU is Springer Nature Customer Service Centre GmbH, Europaplatz 3, 69115 Heidelberg, Germany. If you have any concerns regarding our products, please contact ProductSafety@springernature.com

Printed and bound by CPI Group (UK) Ltd, Croydon, CR0 4YY
30/09/2026
02225258-0003